CREATIVE COOKING COLLECTION

Food Processor Cooking

CREATIVE COOKING COLLECTION

Food Processor Cooking

Carol Bowen

CONTENTS

Published exclusively for Cupress (Canada) Limited
10 Falconer Drive, Unit 8, Mississauga,
Ontario L5N 1B1, Canada
by Woodhead-Faulkner Ltd

First published 1987
© Woodhead-Faulkner (Publishers) Ltd 1987
All rights reserved
ISBN 0-920691-12-9
Printed and bound in Singapore

INTRODUCTION

If you're the sort of cook who hesitates to try a recipe because it calls for a finely chopped ingredient, a food to be puréed, sieved or grated finely, then you will have warmly welcomed the recent arrival of the food processor, which will easily and speedily dispense with those arduous and muscle-aching food preparation chores, opening new doors to delicious meals.

However, with availability has also come variety—and the decision of which processor to buy has become more complex. Size, features, price and performance are just some of the important considerations. Every food processor will mix, grind, slice, shred, blend, knead, grate, purée and chop at the very minimum using the standard metal chopping blade, grating disc and slicing disc attachments provided; many, with optional extras, will do a lot more.

BASIC FOOD PROCESSOR MODELS

There are two basic types of food processor, categorized by the motors they use. Most are powered by a belt-drive motor, with the bowl placed beside the motor. More expensive but more durable is the direct drive motor processor where the bowl usually sits on top of the motor.

Every manufacturer provides the three basic attachments, plus a spatula and feed tube. In addition, the following may also be available:
- plastic blending blade (often a standard too) for mixing doughs, batters, creamed cake mixtures and sauces
- whipping or whisking blade (increasingly becoming a standard attachment) for whipping cream, whisking egg whites and making light-as-air sponges
- French fry or chipper disc
- juice extractor or citrus press
- soft ice cream maker
- dough kit
- Parmesan cheese grater disc
- ripple-cut disc

Some models also offer a wider selection of the basic attachments: fine, medium or coarse grater; thin or thick slicer; and even a special coleslaw grater disc. Use different discs, if you have them, to provide a variety of shapes and textures—particularly important in salads and vegetable dishes. Many manufacturers will take separate orders for an additional bowl—a very useful extra that helps cut down on annoying mid-recipe bowl rinsing.

Many processors simply work on one speed, but with some the speed can be increased by turning a dial or pressing a button. A pulse button—where action can be added at the touch of a finger—is a good feature to look out for, as it gives very precise control when processing small quantities or delicate items.

With the trend towards co-ordinated kitchens, food processors now come in a variety of colours and, if you're planning a new kitchen, one model can be built into a worktop for convenience.

EFFICIENT USE

Having chosen the best processor for your requirements, the next considera-
tion is how to use it most efficiently. Processors are the new 'merlins' of the
kitchen, but their wizardry can go haywire if you don't observe a few basic
rules, which I call the 'three Rs':

Right Order: There is a logical order to processing foods. It comes quickly and
naturally with use but as a general guide:

- process foods that require a dry bowl first, then remove
- secondly, slice or grate any foods that need to be incorporated into chopped
mixtures later; remove
- next process foods that require a long chopping time
- follow with delicate foods that require short chopping times to give an
overall uniform mixture
- finally blend or mix any items together

Right Time: Speed is one of the major features of the food processor but
timings are critical. Follow the recipe guidelines exactly or err on the side of
safety by under-processing, adding extra action via the pulse button if your
model has one. It's only too easy to end up with a vegetable purée instead of
chopped vegetables if you don't keep an eye on what's happening.

Right Load: Processing more than the ideal load for your processor will not
save time but simply strain the motor and give uneven results. It is easier and
safer to process in batches. Ideal load capacities for the standard model used in
this book are:

- 1 kg (2 lb) bread dough—to make and knead
- 600 ml (2½ cups) cooked vegetables and stock—to purée for soup
- 500 g (1 lb) meat—for chopping or grinding
- 4-egg Victoria sandwich—to mix
- 625 g (1¼ lb) shortcrust pastry—to mix
- 600 ml (2½ cups) mayonnaise—to make

SAFETY AND CARE

Never immerse the motor base in water—simply wipe with a damp cloth.

Never leave blades and discs to soak in water for unsuspecting hands.

Never use fingers, spoons or other implements instead of the special pusher
provided for use with the feed tube.

Make sure that the bowl is safely locked into position before fitting attachments
and before switching on.

Don't attempt to touch the food before the blade has stopped; a safety lock will
ensure that the motor stops when the lid is opened, but the blade takes a little
longer to stop unless you have a model with a blade brake.

PROCESSOR SHORT-CUT TIPS

- Make speedy long-lasting garlic purée in bulk. Fit the metal chopping blade.
Place about 20 cloves garlic in the processor bowl with a pinch of salt
and process for about 20 seconds, until smooth, scraping down once. Add
2 tablespoons oil and process for 5 seconds. Place in a screw-topped jar
and cover with a little oil. Store in the refrigerator for up to 2 months. Use
½–1 teaspoon purée for each garlic clove required.

- Make fresh breadcrumbs speedily. Fit the metal chopping blade, then, with the motor running, add bread cubes through the feed tube and process for 5–8 seconds.
- Chop herbs for use in salads, savoury dishes and garnishing. Fit the metal chopping blade. Place the herbs in the processor bowl or, with the motor running, add through the feed tube. Process for 3–6 seconds, to chop to desired fineness. Bag and freeze if you wish.
- Be economical with oddments like cheese. Grate or slice in the processor and freeze in plastic bags for instant use in sauces, toppings, etc.
- Slice halved or quartered citrus fruits in bulk. Freeze and use for drinks and garnishes.
- Make chocolate decorations for cakes and desserts, using the grating disc. Chocolate at room temperature will give curls; hard chocolate will give chips.
- Chop nuts speedily: fit the metal chopping blade and process for 2–5 seconds to desired fineness.

RECIPE GUIDELINES

All the recipes and timings given in this book refer to a standard 1.8 litre (7½ cup) food processor model with just the three basic attachments—metal chopping blade, medium slicing disc and grating disc; notes are given for use of optional extras where applicable.

It is important to note that, before adding directly to the processor bowl, carrots, celery, zucchini and bananas should be cut into 2 or 3 large pieces, depending on their size; cucumbers, peppers and onions, except small ones, should be quartered; meat should be cut roughly into 5 cm (2 inch) squares. This will aid the chopping or mincing process.

Foods to be sliced or grated should be cut into pieces to fit into the feed tube and pushed down to the disc with the pusher.

Ingredients are introduced in the right order for maximum efficiency and all processing has been timed accurately for the best results.

Only wash the food processor bowl during a recipe if it says so—if it isn't stated, it isn't necessary.

NOTES

Ingredients are given in both metric and imperial measures. Use either set of quantities but not a mixture of both in any one recipe.

All spoon measurements are level:
1 tablespoon = one 15 ml spoon
1 teaspoon = one 5 ml spoon

Ovens should be preheated to the temperature specified.

Freshly ground black pepper is intended where pepper is listed.

Fresh herbs are used unless otherwise stated. If unobtainable, dried herbs can be substituted in cooked dishes but halve the quantities.

Eggs are large size unless otherwise stated.

Basic recipes are marked with an asterisk and given on pages 76–9. Increase or decrease the basic quantities in proportion to obtain the amount required.

SMOKED TROUT PÂTÉ

A delicious creamy pâté that freezes so well it is worth making in bulk. Thaw in the refrigerator overnight or at room temperature for 4–6 hours.

500 g (1 lb) smoked trout, skinned and boned
125 g (4 oz) butter, softened
1 tablespoon lemon juice

1 tablespoon creamed horseradish
salt and pepper to taste
TO GARNISH:
lemon twists
parsley sprigs

Serves 6
Preparation time: 10 minutes, plus chilling
Freezing: Recommended

1. Fit the metal chopping blade. Place the trout and butter in the processor bowl and process for 10–15 seconds, until smooth.
2. Add the lemon juice, horseradish, and salt and pepper and process for about 5 seconds, until smooth and creamy.
3. Spoon into 6 individual dishes and chill until firm.
4. Garnish with lemon twists and parsley and serve with toast or savoury crackers.

CREAMY TARAMASALATA

This popular Greek appetizer is delicious served with crusty bread, pitta bread or toast. It can also be used as a spread for canapés or a dip for vegetable sticks.

125 g (4 oz) smoked cods' roe, skinned
4 slices bread, crusts removed and cubed
3 tablespoons lemon juice

1 clove garlic
150 ml (2/3 cup) olive oil
TO GARNISH:
black olives
lemon slices

Serves 6–8
Preparation time: 10 minutes
Freezing: Not recommended

1. Fit the metal chopping blade. Place the cods' roe, bread, lemon juice and garlic in the processor bowl and process for 10–15 seconds, until smooth; scrape down the bowl if necessary halfway through processing.
2. With the motor running, slowly pour the oil through the feed tube, and process for about 1 second, to mix.
3. Spoon into a small serving bowl and garnish with black olives and lemon slices.

TRADITIONAL FARMHOUSE PÂTÉ

*250 g (8 oz) bacon
  slices*
*250 g (8 oz) pork shoulder
  steak*
250 g (8 oz) pigs' liver
*250 g (8 oz) pork
  sausagemeat*

1 small onion
1 clove garlic
*¹/₂ teaspoon dried
  marjoram*
salt and pepper to taste

Serves 8–10
Preparation time:
20 minutes, plus
chilling
Cooking time:
1½–1¾ hours
Freezing:
Recommended

1. Stretch the bacon with a palette knife and use two thirds of the slices to line a 500 g (1 lb) loaf tin.
2. Fit the metal chopping blade. Place the pork in the processor bowl and process for about 5 seconds, until finely chopped.
3. Add the remaining ingredients and process for 6–8 seconds, until finely chopped. Place in the tin, smoothing the top. Cover with the remaining bacon.
4. Cover with foil and place in a roasting tin half-filled with hot water. Cook in a preheated oven, 170°C/325°F, for 1½–1¾ hours, until firm.
5. Replace the foil with waxed paper, place a 1 kg (2 lb) weight on top and leave until cold. Chill overnight.
6. Turn out, slice and serve with toast and salad.

POTTED CHEESE RESERVE

Potted cheese is an old English favourite that has earned a fine reputation. Use any variety or a mixture of the great English cheeses—mature Cheddar, Stilton, Cheshire, Caerphilly, Lancashire, Wensleydale, Red Leicester, Double Gloucester or Derby.

250 g (8 oz) English cheese
  (see above)
75 g (3 oz) unsalted butter,
  softened

1 tablespoon snipped
  chives
2 tablespoons port
pinch of cayenne pepper
walnut halves to garnish

1. Fit the grating disc and grate the cheese; remove and set aside.
2. Fit the metal chopping or plastic blending blade. Place the butter, cheese, chives, port and cayenne pepper in the processor bowl and process for 3–5 seconds, to blend thoroughly.
3. Spoon into a terrine or 4 small serving dishes, cover and chill for 1 hour.
4. Garnish with walnut halves and serve with savoury crackers, crispbreads or celery.

Serves 4
Preparation time:
10–15 minutes,
plus chilling
Freezing:
Recommended for
up to 1 month

CHICKEN AND BRANDY MOUSSE

One of the easiest mousses to make, yet one whose flavour belies such simplicity. Garnish with an elegant centrepiece, e.g. orange segments or edible nasturtium flowers, tossed with watercress sprigs or shredded radicchio.

70 g (2½ oz) packet aspic jelly powder
600 ml (2½ cups) very hot chicken stock
250 g (8 oz) smoked chicken, skinned
1 tablespoon tomato paste

1 teaspoon chopped parsley
2 egg yolks
250 ml (1 cup) whipping cream
125 ml (½ cup) brandy
pepper to taste

Serves 6–8
Preparation time: 15 minutes, plus chilling
Freezing: Recommended

1. Place the aspic in a bowl, gradually add the very hot stock and whisk well until dissolved. Leave until cool but not set.
2. Fit the metal chopping blade. Place the cooled aspic and remaining ingredients in the processor bowl and process for about 20 seconds, until smooth and creamy.
3. Spoon into an oiled 1.2 litre (5 cup) fluted ring mould and chill until set.
4. To serve, dip briefly into hot water, turn out onto a serving dish and fill the centre with a salad garnish.

CRAB AND CUCUMBER MOUSSE

This fresh, light mousse makes a stunning cold buffet centrepiece if set in a fish-shaped or fluted ring mould.

175 g (6 oz) cucumber
1 envelope gelatine, soaked in 3 tablespoons water
250 g (8 oz) crab meat, flaked
150 ml (²/₃ cup) Mayonnaise*
1 tablespoon lemon juice

1 tablespoon tomato ketchup
dash of Tabasco sauce
²/₃ cup whipping cream
salt and pepper to taste
cucumber slices to garnish

1. Fit the metal chopping blade. Peel the cucumber, place in the processor bowl and process for about 1 second, to chop. Remove and set aside.
2. Heat the gelatine gently until dissolved.
3. Place the crab meat, gelatine, mayonnaise, lemon juice, tomato ketchup, Tabasco sauce, and salt and pepper in the

processor bowl and process for about 20 seconds, until smooth.

4. Add the cucumber and process for 1 second, to mix.

5. Whip the cream until it stands in soft peaks (using the processor whipping blade if your model has one), then fold into the crab mixture with a metal spoon.

6. Spoon into an oiled 900 ml (3⅔ cup) decorative fish or fluted ring mould and chill until set.

7. To serve, dip briefly into hot water, turn out onto a serving dish and garnish with cucumber.

Serves 6
Preparation time:
30 minutes, plus chilling
Freezing:
Not recommended

THREE DIP CRUDITÉS

Crisp vegetable sticks served with a variety of dips make a delicious stand-up starter to serve with drinks.

DEVILLED HAM DIP:
¼ onion
¼ red pepper
25 g (1 oz) ham
6 tablespoons
  *Mayonnaise**
2 tablespoons corn relish
½ teaspoon mustard
salt and pepper to taste
WATERCRESS AND
  ORANGE DIP:
½ bunch watercress
flesh of ½ orange
8 tablespoons
  *Mayonnaise**
1 tablespoon orange juice
1 teaspoon finely grated
  orange rind
salt and pepper to taste

COOL AVOCADO DIP:
½ small ripe avocado
2 teaspoons lemon juice
8 tablespoons
  *Mayonnaise**
1 tablespoon chopped
  parsley
salt and pepper to taste
VEGETABLE CRUDITÉS:
4 large carrots
¼ cucumber
1 red and 1 green or
  yellow pepper, cored
  and seeded
TO SERVE:
about 18 olives
about 18 button
  mushrooms
crisp savoury crackers

Serves 4–6
Preparation time:
20–25 minutes
Freezing:
Not recommended

Devilled Ham Dip
Fit the metal chopping blade. Place the onion, red pepper and ham in the processor bowl and process for 3–4 seconds, until finely chopped. Add the remaining ingredients and process for 1–2 seconds, to blend. Spoon into a small bowl, cover and chill until required.

Watercress and Orange Dip
Fit the metal chopping blade. Place the watercress in the processor bowl and process for 1–2 seconds, until coarsely chopped. Add the remaining ingredients and process for about 2 seconds, until blended. Spoon into a small bowl, cover and chill until required.

Cool Avocado Dip
Fit the metal chopping blade. Place all the ingredients in the processor bowl and process for about 5 seconds, until smooth. Spoon into a bowl, cover and chill until required.

Vegetable Crudités
Fit the slicing disc and slice the vegetables. (Or use a chipper or French fry disc if your processor has one.)

To Serve:
Arrange the crudités on a large platter with the olives, mushrooms and savoury crackers. Serve with the dips.

MUSTARD AND SOUR CREAM DIP

A delicious, creamy yet crunchy, dip to serve with smoked
fish as a starter.

1 apple, cored
1 teaspoon lemon juice
4 green onions
1 cup sour cream

2–3 teaspoons French
*   mustard*
salt and pepper to taste

1. Fit the grating disc and grate the apple. Place in a mixing
bowl. Add the lemon juice and toss well.
2. Fit the metal chopping blade. Place the green onions in
the processor bowl and process for 2–3 seconds, until
coarsely chopped. Set aside about 2 teaspoons for garnish.
3. Add all the remaining ingredients to the processor
bowl and process for 1–2 seconds, to blend.
4. Spoon into a small bowl and sprinkle with the reserved
chopped green onion. Cover and chill in the refrigerator
until required.
5. Serve with smoked mackerel or trout.

Serves 4
Preparation time:
10 minutes
Freezing:
Not recommended

BACON AND SPLIT PEA SOUP

*50 g (2 oz) salt pork
or bacon
1 large onion
25 g (1 oz) butter
125 g (4 oz) yellow split
peas*

*900 ml (3²/₃ cups) light
stock
pepper to taste
chopped parsley to garnish*

Serves 4
Preparation time:
10 minutes
Cooking time:
1½ hours
Freezing:
Recommended

1. Fit the metal chopping blade. Place the bacon in the processor bowl and process for 3–4 seconds, to chop. Remove and set aside.
2. Add the onion to the processor bowl and process for 2–3 seconds, until finely chopped.
3. Melt the butter in a large heavy-based pan, add the onion and bacon and fry for 5 minutes, until softened.
4. Add the split peas and stock, cover and bring to the boil, then simmer for 1½ hours, stirring occasionally. Cool slightly.
5. Purée the soup in the processor bowl, in batches if necessary, for about 8 seconds per batch.
6. Return to the pan, season with pepper and heat gently.
7. Pour into a warmed tureen, garnish with parsley and serve with crusty bread.

CLASSIC SPANISH GAZPACHO

*3 small slices whole wheat
  bread, cubed
600 ml (2¹/₂ cups) tomato
  juice
1 green and 1 red pepper,
  cored and seeded
¹/₂ cucumber
1 large onion
750 g (1¹/₂ lb) tomatoes,
  skinned and seeded*

*2 cloves garlic
4 tablespoons olive oil
2 tablespoons red wine
  vinegar
¹/₂ teaspoon dried basil
salt and pepper to taste
TO SERVE:
croûtons
chopped onion, pepper,
  olives and cucumber*

1. Place the bread in a bowl, pour over the tomato juice and leave for 5 minutes. Remove the bread, squeezing to extract the juice, and set aside. Reserve the tomato juice.
2. Fit the metal chopping blade. Place the bread, peppers, cucumber, onion, tomatoes and garlic in the processor bowl and process, in batches if necessary, for about 20 seconds per batch, until smooth.
3. Add all the remaining ingredients and process, in batches, for 3–5 seconds per batch, to blend. Pour into a tureen and chill for at least 1 hour.
4. Serve with bowls of croûtons, and chopped onion, pepper, olives and cucumber, for sprinkling on the soup.

Serves 4–6
Preparation time:
15 minutes, plus
chilling
Freezing:
Not recommended

WATERCRESS SOUP

A tasty fresh-looking soup, equally good served hot with crusty bread or chilled.

2 bunches watercress	*450 ml (1¾ cups)*
1 onion	*vegetable stock*
2 tablespoons butter	*450 ml (1¾ cups) milk*
500 g (1 lb) potatoes,	*⅔ cup cream*
chopped	*salt and pepper to taste*

Serves 6
Preparation time:
15 minutes
Cooking time:
40 minutes
Freezing:
Recommended at
end of stage 6

1. Discard the lower stalks from the watercress.
2. Fit the metal chopping blade. Place the watercress in the processor bowl and process for 2–3 seconds, until coarsely chopped. Remove and set aside.
3. Add the onion to the processor bowl and process for 2–3 seconds, until finely chopped.
4. Melt the butter in a pan, add the onion and watercress, cover and cook gently for 5 minutes.
5. Add the potatoes, stock, milk, and salt and pepper, bring to the boil, then cover and simmer for 35 minutes. Cool slightly.
6. Purée the soup in the processor bowl, in batches if necessary, for about 8 seconds per batch.
7. To serve hot, return the soup to the pan, stir in the cream and heat gently. Pour into individual warmed soup bowls.
8. To serve cold, pour into individual soup bowls and chill. Swirl a spoonful of cream on top of each just before serving.

BRANDIED FRENCH ONION SOUP

A classic French onion soup prepared the 'no-tears' way in the processor. The addition of brandy and floating cheese croûte garnish makes it a sophisticated soup for serving at a dinner party.

500 g (1 lb) onions	*125 g (4 oz) Gruyère or*
¼ cup butter	*Emmenthal cheese*
1 tablespoon oil	*4 thick slices French bread*
½ teaspoon light brown	*2 teaspoons snipped chives*
soft sugar	*2 tablespoons brandy*
2 tablespoons flour	*salt and pepper to taste*
1 litre (4 cups) rich beef	
stock	

1. Fit the slicing disc and slice the onions.
2. Heat the butter and oil in a large heavy-based pan, add the onions, cover and cook for 20 minutes.
3. Stir in the sugar, increase the heat and cook for 5–10 minutes, until the onions turn a rich golden colour, stirring frequently.
4. Stir in the flour and cook until browned, then gradually add the stock. Season with salt and pepper. Bring to the boil, then cover and simmer for 20 minutes.
5. Meanwhile, fit the grating disc and grate the cheese.
6. Toast the bread on one side, turn and sprinkle with the cheese; broil until bubbling. Sprinkle with the chives.
7. Add the brandy to the soup and reheat gently. Pour into warmed soup bowls and top each with a cheese croûte.

Serves 4
Preparation time: 15 minutes
Cooking time: 45–50 minutes
Freezing: Recommended, without the croûtes

PORK WITH ORCHARD STUFFING

2 parsley sprigs
2 slices bread, cubed
1 small onion
1 celery stick
1 apple, peeled, cored and quartered
50 g (2 oz) cashew nuts
2 tablespoons butter
2 teaspoons lemon juice

1.75 kg (4 lb) loin of pork, boned and scored
FOR THE SAUCE:
2 teaspoons corn starch
150 ml (²/₃ cup) pure apple juice or cider
1 tablespoon whipping cream
salt and pepper to taste

Serves 6
Preparation time:
15 minutes
Cooking time:
About 2½ hours
Freezing:
Not recommended

1. Fit the metal chopping blade. With the motor running, add the parsley and bread through the feed tube and process for about 5 seconds, to make herby crumbs. Remove and set aside.
2. Place the onion and celery in the processor bowl and process for 3–4 seconds, to chop. Remove and set aside.
3. Place the apple in the processor bowl and process for 2–3 seconds, to chop. Remove and set aside.
4. Add the nuts to the processor bowl and process for 2–3 seconds, until coarsely chopped. Remove and set aside.
5. Melt the butter in a pan, add the celery and onion mixture and cook gently for 5 minutes. Add the apple and nuts and cook for 3 minutes. Add the breadcrumbs, lemon juice, and salt and pepper and mix well. Place the mixture along the pork loin, roll up and tie firmly. Brush with oil and rub with salt.
6. Weigh the roast and calculate the cooking time, allowing 30 minutes per 500 g (1 lb), plus 30 minutes. Place on a rack in a roasting pan and cook in a preheated oven, 180°C/350°F, for the calculated time; raise the oven temperature to 220°C/425°F for the last 10 minutes to crisp the crackling. Keep warm while preparing the sauce.
7. Skim away any fat from the meat juices. Place the corn starch in a small pan, gradually add the meat juices and blend well. Gradually add the apple juice or cider and bring to the boil, stirring constantly, until smooth and thickened. Stir in the cream and salt and pepper.
8. Slice the pork and serve immediately, with the sauce and seasonal vegetables.

SWEET AND SOUR PORK BALLS

Delicious balls of pork simmered in a rich and colourful sweet and sour sauce make this dish exotic enough to serve at a dinner party, with plain boiled rice and a crisp green salad.

pared rind of ¼ orange
3 slices brown bread,
*   cubed*
750 g (1½ lb) diced pork
1 large onion
dash of Tabasco sauce
1 egg
2 tablespoons oil
salt and pepper to taste
parsley or coriander sprigs
*   to garnish*
FOR THE SAUCE:
1 each green, red and
*   yellow pepper, cored*
*   and seeded*

1 tablespoon corn starch
175 ml (¾ cup) stock
1 tablespoon oil
2 tomatoes, skinned and
*   chopped*
3 tablespoons light brown
*   soft sugar*
1 tablespoon soy sauce
3 tablespoons red wine
*   vinegar*
175 ml (¾ cup) pure
*   orange juice*
½ teaspoon Chinese
*   5-spice powder*

Serves 6
Preparation time:
25 minutes
Cooking time:
30–35 minutes
Freezing:
Recommended

1. Fit the metal chopping blade. With the motor running, add the orange rind then the bread cubes through the feed tube and process for 5–8 seconds, to make citrus-flavoured crumbs. Remove and set aside.
2. Place the pork in the processor bowl and process for 4–6 seconds, to mince.
3. Add the onion, breadcrumbs, Tabasco sauce, egg, and salt and pepper and process for 4–6 seconds, to mix. Remove the mixture and shape into about 18–20 meatballs.
4. Heat the oil in a heavy-based frying pan, add the pork balls and fry for about 10 minutes, until evenly browned.
5. Meanwhile, prepare the sauce. Place the peppers in the processor bowl and process for 4–5 seconds, to chop.
6. Place the corn starch in a small bowl, add a little of the stock and mix until smooth. Gradually stir in the remaining stock and set aside.
7. Heat the oil in another pan, add the peppers, and fry for about 5 minutes, until softened. Add the blended corn starch with the remaining ingredients and salt and pepper. Bring to the boil, stirring, then pour over the pork balls.
8. Cover and cook gently for 20–25 minutes, until the pork balls are tender and the sauce has thickened. Garnish with parsley or coriander to serve.

CHEESY TOAD-IN-THE-HOLES

*125 g (4 oz) Cheddar
    cheese
1 tablespoon oil
500 g (1 lb) pork sausages*

*¹/₂–1 teaspoon mustard
300 ml (1¹/₄ cups) Basic
    Batter*
sage leaves to garnish*

1. Fit the grating disc and grate the cheese.
2. Divide the oil and sausages between 8 small Yorkshire pudding tins or place in 1 large 20 × 30 cm (8 × 12 inch) shallow ovenproof dish. Cook in a preheated oven, 220°C/425°F, for 10 minutes (if using the small cocktail sausages, cook for only 5 minutes). Lower the oven temperature to 200°C/400°F.
3. Add the mustard and half the cheese to the batter, pour around the sausages and sprinkle with remaining cheese.
4. Bake for 20–30 minutes, until well risen, crisp and golden brown. Serve immediately, garnished with sage.

Serves 4
Preparation time:
10 minutes, plus
making batter
Cooking time:
25–40 minutes
Freezing:
Not recommended

PORK AND KUMQUAT CURRY

Kumquats add elegance to this curry, but if unavailable
substitute thin-skinned clementines, or cubed mango.

*750 g (1½ lb) pork
tenderloin
1 large onion
2 tablespoons oil
2 bay leaves
2 cardamoms
6 cloves
6 black peppercorns
½ teaspoon ground
cumin
1 cinnamon stick
2 tablespoons tomato
paste
250 ml (1 cup) stock*

*250 ml (1 cup) pure
orange juice
250 g (8 oz) kumquats,
quartered
FOR THE CURRY PASTE:
1 onion
1 clove garlic
1 tablespoon coriander
seeds
1 teaspoon ground ginger
1 teaspoon chilli powder
2 teaspoons garam masala
1½ teaspoons turmeric*

Serves 4–6
Preparation time:
20–25 minutes
Cooking time:
45–50 minutes
Freezing:
Recommended
for up to 1 month

1. First, make the curry paste. Fit the metal chopping
blade. Place all the ingredients in the processor bowl and
process for about 20 seconds, to purée. Set aside.
2. Fit the slicing disc and slice the onion.
3. Cut the pork into cubes. Heat the oil in a flameproof
casserole, add the onion and pork and cook over a high
heat for about 10 minutes, until evenly browned.
4. Add the bay leaves, cardamoms, cloves, peppercorns,
cumin, cinnamon stick, tomato paste, stock and orange
juice and mix well. Cover and simmer for 10 minutes.
5. Stir in the kumquats and curry paste, blending well.
Cover and simmer for 25–30 minutes, until very tender.
6. Serve with Basmati rice and a cucumber salad.

TURKEY BREASTS SURPRISE

Turkey breasts are an economical way of buying prime
turkey meat for a tasty family supper dish.

*2 slices day-old bread,
cubed
1 teaspoon dried Herbes de
Provence
75 g (3 oz) Cheddar cheese
4 turkey breasts
4 slices ham*

*4 teaspoons mustard
1 egg, beaten
¼ cup butter
1 tablespoon oil
salt and pepper to taste
thyme sprigs to garnish*

1. Fit the metal chopping blade. With the motor running, add the bread cubes through the feed tube and process for about 5 seconds, to make fine dry breadcrumbs. Add the herbs, and salt and pepper and process for about 1 second, to mix. Place in a shallow dish.
2. Fit the grating disc and grate the cheese.
3. Flatten the turkey breasts by hitting with a rolling pin or meat mallet. Spread one side of each breast with mustard, top with grated cheese and cover with a slice of ham.
4. Carefully dip the turkey breasts into the beaten egg, then coat in the breadcrumbs, patting well to seal.
5. Heat the butter and oil in a heavy-based frying pan, add the turkey breasts and fry for about 15 minutes, turning once, until golden and cooked through. Drain on kitchen paper.
6. Garnish with thyme and serve immediately, with baked tomatoes or Vegetable Mirepoix (page 34).

Serves 4
Preparation time:
20 minutes
Cooking time:
15 minutes
Freezing:
Recommended at end of stage 4; thaw thoroughly before cooking

VEGETABLES TAJ MAHAL

Fresh coconut gives this a wonderful flavour; but you could use 65 g (2½ oz) creamed coconut, blended with 175 ml (¾ cup) hot water, to replace coconut and water.

5 cm (2 inch) piece fresh root ginger	*1½ teaspoons turmeric*
2 cloves garlic	*2 teaspoons garam masala*
1 onion	*1 tablespoon ground coriander*
1 green chilli, seeded	*125 g (4 oz) green beans*
2 carrots	*125 g (4 oz) cauliflower florets*
2 celery sticks	*2 potatoes, diced*
1 small egg plant, quartered	*50 g (2 oz) okra*
1 green pepper, cored and seeded	*50 g (2 oz) button onions*
4 tablespoons oil	*1 teaspoon salt*
1 teaspoon mustard seeds, crushed	*250 g (8 oz) fresh coconut flesh*
	175 ml (¾ cup) water

Serves 4
Preparation time: 20 minutes
Cooking time: About 45 minutes
Freezing: Recommended for up to 1 month

1. Fit the metal chopping blade. Place the ginger, garlic, onion and chilli in the processor bowl and process for 8–10 seconds, until finely chopped. Remove and set aside.
2. Fit the slicing disc and slice the carrots, celery, egg plant and green pepper. Remove and set aside.
3. Heat the oil in a large pan, add the mustard seeds and fry for 1 minute. Stir in the onion mixture and fry gently for 10 minutes. Add the turmeric, garam masala and coriander and cook for 2 minutes. Add all the vegetables, stir well and cook gently for 5 minutes.
4. Meanwhile, fit the metal chopping blade. Place the salt, coconut and water in the processor bowl and process for about 20 seconds, to purée. Add to the vegetable mixture, cover and simmer for 25 minutes.
5. Spoon into a warmed serving dish. Serve with Basmati rice, poppadoms, yogurt and mango pickle.

BACON GOUGÈRE

75 g (3 oz) Cheddar cheese	*2-egg quantity Choux Pastry**
1 onion	*2 tablespoons fresh breadcrumbs (see page 7)*
175 g (6 oz) cooked bacon or ham	*salt and pepper to taste*
125 g (4 oz) mushrooms	
1 tablespoon oil	

1. Fit the grating disc and grate the cheese. Remove and set aside.

2. Fit the metal chopping blade. Place the onion and bacon or ham in the processor bowl and process for 3–4 seconds, until coarsely chopped. Set aside.

3. Fit the slicing disc and slice the mushrooms.

4. Heat the oil in a pan, add the onion mixture, mushrooms, and salt and pepper, and cook gently for 8–10 minutes, stirring occasionally.

5. Add 50 g (2 oz) of the cheese to the choux pastry and process for 5–10 seconds, to mix.

6. Spoon half of the pastry into a greased 1.2 litre (5 cup) ovenproof dish or, for individual portions, divide between 4 large scallop shells. Spoon the bacon mixture into the centre.

7. Spoon or pipe the remaining pastry around the edge and sprinkle with the remaining cheese. Sprinkle the bacon filling with the breadcrumbs.

8. Bake in a preheated oven, 200°C/400°F, for 40–45 minutes; for individual dishes bake for 25–30 minutes. Serve immediately.

Serves 4
Preparation time: 30 minutes, plus making pastry
Cooking time: 25–45 minutes
Freezing: Not recommended

SHRIMP AND WATERCRESS FLAN

250 g (8 oz) Lemon
   Shortcrust Pastry*
1 small onion
1 bunch watercress
1 tablespoon butter
3 extra large eggs,
   beaten

²⁄₃ cup cream
2 teaspoons mustard
   powder
125 g (4 oz) peeled shrimp
salt and pepper to taste

Serves 4–6
Preparation time:
20–25 minutes,
plus making pastry
Cooking time:
35–40 minutes
Freezing:
Not recommended

1. Roll out the prepared pastry on a lightly floured surface and use to line a 23 cm (9 inch) loose-based flan tin. Line with waxed paper and fill with baking beans. Bake 'blind' in a preheated oven, 190°C/375°F, for 15 minutes. Lower the temperature to 180°C/350°F.
2. Meanwhile, fit the metal chopping blade. Place the onion and watercress in the processor bowl and process for about 5 seconds, to chop.
3. Melt the butter in a pan, add the onion and watercress and cook gently for 5 minutes. Remove from the heat, leave to cool slightly, then stir in the eggs, cream, mustard, and salt and pepper.
4. Remove the waxed paper and beans from the flan case and sprinkle the shrimp over the base. Pour in the watercress mixture. Return to the oven and bake for 20–25 minutes, until firm. Remove the flan from the tin.
5. Serve warm or cold with a mixed salad, for a special family lunch or supper dish.

TURKEY PICNIC PIE

A veal, ham and turkey raised pie makes a splendid centrepiece for any cold spread. Serve on a picnic, as part of a cold buffet, or as a lunchbox item.

250 g (8 oz) stewing veal
250 g (8 oz) cooked ham
1 onion
pinch of ground mace or
   grated nutmeg
350 g (12 oz) Hot Water
   Crust Pastry*
300 g (10 oz) cooked
   turkey, diced

salt and pepper to taste
beaten egg or milk
   to glaze
FOR THE JELLIED STOCK:
300 ml (1¼ cups) chicken
   stock
1 envelope gelatine

1. Fit the metal chopping blade. Place the veal, ham, onion, mace or nutmeg, and salt and pepper in the processor bowl and process for 15–20 seconds, to chop finely or mince.

2. Roll out two thirds of the pastry on a lightly floured surface and use to line a greased 15 cm (6 inch) round loose-bottomed cake tin or small game pie mould.

3. Place half of the veal mixture in the tin, cover with the turkey and top with the remaining veal mixture.

4. Roll out the remaining pastry to make a lid. Dampen the pastry rim and cover with the lid. Trim, seal and flute the edges. Use any pastry trimmings to decorate the pie as you wish. Make a hole in the top of the pie and place on a baking sheet. Brush with beaten egg or milk.

5. Bake in a preheated oven, 200°C/400°F, for 30 minutes. Lower the temperature to 170°C/325°F, glaze again and bake for 1–1¼ hours. Leave in the tin to cool.

6. To make the jellied stock, place the stock and gelatine in a pan and heat gently until dissolved. Season with salt and pepper, leave to cool, then pour gradually through a funnel into the pie through the hole in the lid. Chill overnight. Remove from the tin to serve.

Serves 8
Preparation time:
20–30 minutes,
plus making pastry
and chilling
Cooking time:
1½–1¾ hours
Freezing:
Not recommended

SUPPER PIZZAS

FOR THE BASE:
250 ml (2 cups) all-
    purpose flour
1 teaspoon salt
2 tablespoons butter
150 ml (²/₃ cup) milk or
    milk and water mixed
FOR THE TOPPING:
1 onion
1 teaspoon dried oregano
1 teaspoon dried basil

1 teaspoon sugar
2 × 397 g (14 oz) cans
    tomatoes, drained
250 g (8 oz) Mozzarella
    cheese
4 teaspoons mild burger
    mustard
16 slices salami
4 black olives
salt and pepper to taste

Serves 4
Preparation time:
25–30 minutes
Cooking time:
15 minutes
Freezing:
Recommended at
end of stage 6

1. To make the base, fit the metal chopping blade. Place the flour, salt and butter in the processor bowl and process for 5–7 seconds, until the mixture resembles breadcrumbs.
2. With the motor running, add the milk through the feed tube and process for about 4 seconds, until the mixture forms a smooth dough.
3. Divide the dough into 4 pieces and roll each piece out on a lightly floured surface to a 15 cm (6 inch) round. Place on baking sheets.
4. To make the topping, place the onion in the processor bowl and process for 2–3 seconds, to chop. Place in a pan with the herbs, sugar, tomatoes, and salt and pepper and stir well. Cook for about 15 minutes, until thickened.
5. Meanwhile, fit the grating disc and grate the cheese.
6. Spread 1 teaspoon of the mustard over each pizza base and top with a quarter of the tomato mixture. Cover each with 4 salami slices and sprinkle with a quarter of the cheese. Top each pizza with an olive.
7. Brush with a little olive oil and bake in a preheated oven, 230°C/450°F, for about 15 minutes, until golden and bubbling. Serve piping hot with a green salad.

VARIATIONS

Seafood Supper Pizzas: Prepare as above but replace the salami and olives with 16 canned sardines or 16 anchovy fillets and 175 g (6 oz) peeled shrimp.

Vegetable Supper Pizzas: Prepare as above but replace the salami with 500 g (1 lb) frozen stir-fry vegetables.

Mushroom and Ham Supper Pizzas: Prepare as above but replace the salami and olives with 350 g (12 oz) chopped ham and 350 g (12 oz) sliced mushrooms. Sprinkle with a little chopped oregano before cooking.

VEGETABLES, SALADS & DRESSINGS

LAYERED POTATOES DAUPHINOISE

1 kg (2 lb) potatoes
1 large onion
¼ cup butter

450 ml (1¾ cups) milk
salt and pepper to taste
parsley sprigs to garnish

Serves 4
Preparation time:
15 minutes
Cooking time:
1½–2 hours
Freezing:
Not recommended

1. Fit the slicing disc and slice the potatoes and onion.
2. Lightly grease the base and sides of a large shallow ovenproof dish with some of the butter. Place a layer of potato and onion in the dish, dot with a little butter and sprinkle generously with salt and pepper. Repeat the layers until all the potato and onion has been used. Dot the top with butter.
3. Bring the milk just to the boil, then pour over the potato mixture. Cover with foil and bake in a preheated oven, 190°C/375°F, for 1½–2 hours, removing the foil for the final 45 minutes.
4. Garnish with parsley to serve.

MINTED RATATOUILLE

2 onions
1 green pepper, cored and
* seeded*
1 red or yellow pepper,
* cored and seeded*
250 g (8 oz) zucchini
1 egg plant, quartered
125 g (4 oz) mushrooms

4 tablespoons olive oil
500 g (1 lb) tomatoes,
* skinned, seeded and*
* quartered*
1 tablespoon chopped mint
salt and pepper to taste
mint sprigs to garnish

Serves 4
Preparation time:
20 minutes
Cooking time:
About 1 hour
Freezing:
Recommended

1. Fit the slicing disc and slice the onions, peppers, zucchini and egg plant. Remove and set aside.
2. Slice the mushrooms through the disc and set aside in a separate bowl.
3. Heat the oil in a flameproof casserole, add the onion mixture and fry for about 10 minutes, until softened.
4. Stir in the tomatoes, cover and simmer for 20 minutes.
5. Add the mushrooms, mint, and salt and pepper and stir well. Simmer, uncovered, for about 30 minutes, or until the vegetables are tender but retain their shape.
6. Garnish with mint and serve hot or cold.

VEGETABLE MIREPOIX WITH CITRUS BUTTER

Crisp green vegetables with contrasting flavours and textures make a welcome accompaniment when tossed in a herby lemon butter.

2 celery sticks	*1 sprig each parsley, mint,*
2 zucchini	*tarragon and marjoram*
½ large cucumber	*1 teaspoon snipped chives*
125 g (4 oz) green beans	*2 teaspoons lemon juice*
125 g (4 oz) snow peas	*¼ cup butter*

Serves 4
Preparation time:
15–20 minutes
Cooking time:
5–6 minutes
Freezing:
Not recommended

1. Fit the slicing disc and slice the celery, zucchini and cucumber. Place in a saucepan.
2. Fit the metal chopping blade. Place the green beans in the processor bowl and process for 1–2 seconds, until coarsely chopped. Add to the pan with the snow peas.
3. Cook the vegetables in boiling salted water for 5–6 minutes, until tender but still crisp. Drain thoroughly.
4. Meanwhile, with the motor running, add the herb sprigs through the feed tube and process for about 5 seconds, to chop. Add the chives, lemon juice and butter and process for 8–10 seconds, to blend.
5. Spoon over the hot vegetables and toss well to coat. Serve immediately.

CREAMED SPRING VEGETABLES

A selection of creamed spring vegetables often makes more interesting and enjoyable eating than just plain boiled. For a quick, light supper dish, top with grated cheese and broil until golden and bubbly; serve with crusty bread.

125 g (4 oz) baby carrots	*2 parsley sprigs*
125 g (4 oz) baby turnips	*¼ onion*
2 celery sticks	*2 tablespoons butter*
1 large leek	*¼ cup flour*
125 g (4 oz) spring	*300 ml (1¼ cups) milk*
cabbage	*salt and pepper to taste*
125 g (4 oz) snow peas	*parsley sprigs to garnish*

1. Fit the slicing disc and slice the carrots, turnips, celery and leek. Place in a saucepan and cook in boiling salted water for 10 minutes.

2. Meanwhile, slice the cabbage through the disc. Add to the vegetable mixture with the snow peas and cook for 5 minutes. Drain thoroughly.

3. Meanwhile, fit the metal chopping blade. Place the parsley and onion in the processor bowl and process for 3–4 seconds, until finely chopped.

4. Melt the butter in a pan, add the onion and parsley and cook for 3 minutes. Stir in the flour and cook for 1 minute. Gradually add the milk, bring to the boil, stirring, and cook for 2 minutes. Add the vegetables and toss to coat.

5. Season with salt and pepper and spoon into a warmed serving dish. Serve immediately, garnished with parsley.

Serves 4–6
Preparation time:
20 minutes
Cooking time:
About 15 minutes
Freezing:
Recommended

VEGETABLE PURÉES

500 g (1 lb) parsnips	*GARLIC AND HERB*
500 g (1 lb) carrots	*BUTTER:*
500 g (1 lb) broccoli	*1 clove garlic*
25 g (1 oz) Cheddar	*1 parsley sprig*
cheese, grated (optional)	*¼ cup butter*
BLUE CHEESE BUTTER:	*LEMON AND PARSLEY*
¼ cup butter	*BUTTER:*
50 g (2 oz) blue Stilton	*grated rind of ¼ lemon*
cheese	*1 parsley sprig*
salt and pepper to taste	*¼ cup butter*

Serves 4–6
Preparation time:
30–40 minutes
Cooking time:
10 minutes
Freezing:
Recommended

1. Fit the slicing disc and slice the parsnips. Set aside.
2. Slice the carrots through the disc. Set aside.
3. Split the broccoli into equal-sized spears.
4. Cook the vegetables in separate pans of boiling salted water for about 10 minutes, until tender; drain.
5. Meanwhile, prepare the butters. To prepare the blue cheese butter, fit the metal chopping blade. Place all the ingredients in the processor bowl and process for about 10 seconds, to blend, scraping down the bowl once. Remove and set aside. Wash the processor bowl.
6. To make the garlic and herb butter, fit the metal chopping blade. Place the garlic and parsley in the processor bowl and process for 5–8 seconds, until finely chopped. Add the butter, and salt and pepper to taste and process for 10 seconds, to blend, scraping down the bowl once. Remove and set aside. Wash the processor bowl.
7. To make the lemon and parsley butter, fit the metal chopping blade. Place the lemon rind and parsley in the processor bowl and process for 5–8 seconds, until finely chopped. Add the butter, and salt and pepper to taste and process for about 10 seconds, to blend, scraping down the bowl once. Add the broccoli and process for 3–5 seconds, to purée. Remove and keep warm.
8. Place the parsnips and blue cheese butter in the processor bowl and process for about 5 seconds, to purée. Remove and keep warm.
9. Place the carrots and garlic and herb butter in the processor bowl and process for about 5 seconds, to purée.
10. Serve the vegetable purées in 3 separate warmed dishes, or arrange in a warmed round serving dish to form 3 triangles of colour. Mark the surface with a fork.
11. If you wish, sprinkle with the cheese and cook under a broiler until golden. Serve immediately.

ITALIAN MUSHROOM SALAD

It is essential to use fresh Parmesan cheese for this side salad or starter dish. Slice with the processor slicing disc if your handbook states this is possible, with the special Parmesan cheese grater disc if your model has one, or shave with a sharp knife.

250 g (8 oz) firm white button mushrooms
125 g (4 oz) Parmesan cheese
chopped parsley to garnish

FOR THE VINAIGRETTE:
2 tablespoons lemon juice
1 soft-boiled egg yolk
125 ml (½ cup) salad oil
salt and pepper to taste

Serves 4
Preparation time:
20 minutes
Freezing:
Not recommended

1. Fit the slicing disc and slice the mushrooms. Arrange on a shallow serving plate. Slice the Parmesan (see above) and sprinkle on top.
2. To make the vinaigrette, fit the metal chopping blade. Place the lemon juice, egg yolk, and salt and pepper in the processor bowl and process for about 5 seconds, to blend.
3. With the motor running, pour the oil through the feed tube and process for 4–5 seconds, to make a thickened vinaigrette.
4. Spoon over the salad and sprinkle with parsley. Serve with warm crusty bread.

CUCUMBER AND ZUCCHINI SALAD

A devilled herby vegetable salad, good with cold meats, game pies and other buffet fare. Make at the last possible moment for absolute freshness.

3 small zucchini
1/2 small cucumber
chopped pine nuts to
*   garnish*
FOR THE DRESSING:
6 basil leaves

4 tablespoons salad oil
2 tablespoons white wine
*   vinegar*
1 teaspoon wholegrain
*   mustard*
salt and pepper to taste

1. Fit the grating disc and grate the zucchini and cucumber. Place in a bowl.
2. To make the dressing, fit the metal chopping blade. Place the basil in the processor bowl and process for 2–3 seconds, to chop.
3. Add the oil, vinegar, mustard, and salt and pepper and process for about 3 seconds, to blend.
4. Pour over the cucumber and zucchini and toss to mix.
5. Spoon into a shallow serving dish and sprinkle with chopped pine nuts. Serve immediately.

Serves 4
Preparation time:
10 minutes
Freezing:
Not recommended

WALDORF CELERY CRUNCH

*2 apples, cored and
    quartered
5 celery sticks
75 g (3 oz) roasted salted
    peanuts
398 ml (14 oz) can baby
    corn cobs, drained
1 tablespoon snipped
    chives*

*FOR THE DRESSING:
2 tablespoons sour
    cream
2 tablespoons natural
    yogurt
3 tablespoons natural
    pineapple juice
1 teaspoon dried oregano
pepper to taste*

**Serves 4
Preparation time:**
10–15 minutes
Freezing:
Not recommended

1. Fit the slicing disc and slice the apples and celery. Place in a bowl.
2. Fit the metal chopping blade. Place the peanuts in the processor bowl and process for 2–3 seconds, until coarsely chopped. Add to the apple and celery with the corn cobs and chives, stirring well to mix.
3. To make the dressing, place all the ingredients in the processor bowl and process for 2–3 seconds, to blend. Pour over the salad and toss lightly. Serve immediately.

ROSY COLESLAW

*1 small red cabbage, cored
    and quartered
2 apples, cored and
    quartered
2 celery sticks
3 carrots
½ cup walnut pieces*

*50 g (2 oz) raisins
150 ml (²/₃ cup)
    Mayonnaise*
4 tablespoons natural
    yogurt
salt and cayenne pepper to
    taste*

**Serves 6–8
Preparation time:**
10–15 minutes
Freezing:
Not recommended

1. Fit the slicing disc and slice the cabbage. Place in a serving bowl. Slice the apples and celery through the disc; add to the bowl.
2. Fit the grating disc and grate the carrots. Add to the cabbage mixture with the walnuts and raisins and mix well.
3. Fit the metal chopping or plastic blending blade. Place the mayonnaise, yogurt, and salt and cayenne pepper in the processor bowl and process for about 2 seconds, to blend.
4. Spoon over the coleslaw and toss well to coat. Serve as soon as possible.

CURRIED CHICKEN DISCOVERY

½ cucumber
500 g (1 lb) crisp eating
*   apples, cored and*
*   quartered*
1 large bulb fennel,
*   quartered*
2 tablespoons lemon juice
1.25 kg (2½ lb) chicken,
*   cooked and skinned*

FOR THE DRESSING:
1 quantity Mayonnaise*,
*   made with lemon juice*
2 teaspoons curry paste
2 tablespoons apple sauce
75 ml (⅓ cup) sour
*   cream*
salt and pepper to taste
TO SERVE:
lettuce or chicory leaves

1. Fit the slicing disc and slice the cucumber, apples and fennel. Place in a bowl. Add the lemon juice and toss well. Remove the meat from the chicken, dice and add to the salad; mix well and set aside.
2. Line a serving plate with lettuce or chicory leaves.
3. To make the dressing, fit the metal chopping or plastic blending blade. Place all the ingredients in the processor bowl and process for 3–5 seconds, to mix.
4. Add to the chicken salad, toss carefully, then pile on top of the lettuce or chicory. Serve immediately.

Serves 6
Preparation time:
25 minutes
Freezing:
Not recommended

DELICATESSEN SAUSAGE SALAD

A look along the delicatessen counter will be all the inspiration you need to mix and match the vast array of sausages in this quickly made main meal salad.

2 frankfurters
250 g (8 oz) mixed
  delicatessen sausage, e.g.
  cervelat, salami,
  chorizo, bierwurst,
  mortadella
2 firm ripe pears, peeled
  and quartered
125 g (4 oz) Gruyère
  cheese

chopped parsley to garnish
FOR THE DRESSING:
2 gherkins
1 tablespoon cider or wine
  vinegar
2 teaspoons lemon juice
3 tablespoons salad oil
1/2 teaspoon Dijon
  mustard
salt and pepper to taste

Serves 4
Preparation time:
10–15 minutes
Freezing:
Not recommended

1. Fit the slicing disc and slice the frankfurters. Place in a serving bowl with the other sliced meats.
2. Slice the pears through the disc and add to the sausage mixture.
3. Fit the grating disc and grate the cheese. Add to the sausage mixture.
4. To make the dressing, fit the metal chopping blade. Place the gherkins in the processor bowl and process for about 2 seconds, to chop. Add the remaining ingredients and process for 1–2 seconds, to blend.
5. Pour over the salad and toss quickly to mix. Sprinkle with parsley and serve immediately, with crusty bread.

DANISH BLUE DRESSING

A super blue cheese dressing ideal for salads and sand-wich fillings, and for spooning onto baked potatoes.

125 g (4 oz) Danish blue
  cheese
4 tablespoons
  Mayonnaise*

5 tablespoons natural
  yogurt
pepper to taste
snipped chives to garnish

Makes 300 ml
(1 1/4 cups)
Preparation time:
5 minutes
Freezing:
Not recommended

1. Fit the metal chopping or plastic blending blade. Place the cheese, mayonnaise and yogurt in the processor bowl and process for 8–10 seconds, until smooth and creamy. Transfer to a serving bowl.
2. Season with pepper and chill until required. Sprinkle with chives to serve.

THOUSAND ISLAND DRESSING

1 shallot
2 small gherkins
1/2 each small green and red pepper
10 stuffed green olives
450 ml (1¾ cups) Mayonnaise*

1 tablespoon tomato ketchup
1/4 teaspoon garlic purée (see page 6)
few drops of chilli sauce
salt and pepper to taste
few olive slices to garnish

1. Fit the metal chopping blade. Place the shallot, gherkins, peppers and olives in the processor bowl and process for 3–5 seconds, to chop.
2. Add the mayonnaise, tomato ketchup, garlic purée, chilli sauce, and salt and pepper, and process for 1–2 seconds, to blend.
3. Spoon into a serving dish and top with olive slices. Chill lightly.
4. Serve with salads, as a topping for baked potatoes, or as a hamburger relish.

Makes 600 ml (2½ cups)
Preparation time: 10 minutes
Freezing: Not recommended

DESSERTS

HUMBLE DAMSON CRUMBLE

*750 g (1½ lb) damson
    plums, halved, stoned
    and quartered
2 tablespoons pure orange
    juice
2–4 tablespoons
    dark brown sugar*

*1½ cups whole wheat
    flour
1 teaspoon ground
    cinnamon (optional)
¼ cup butter
¼ cup demerara
    sugar*

Serves 4
Preparation time:
15 minutes
Cooking time:
30 minutes
Freezing:
Recommended

1. Mix the damsons with the orange juice and brown sugar to taste in a 1.2 litre (5 cup) ovenproof dish.
2. Fit the metal chopping blade. Place the flour, cinnamon, if using, and butter in the processor bowl and process for about 6 seconds, until the mixture resembles fine breadcrumbs. Add the demerara sugar and process for about 2 seconds, to mix.
3. Spoon over the damsons, levelling the surface. Bake in a preheated oven, 190°C/375°F, for 30 minutes, until golden.
4. Serve hot with custard, ice cream or whipped cream.

CHERRY KISSEL

*398 ml (14 oz) can black
    cherries, drained and
    stoned
2 tablespoons white wine*

*1 tablespoon lemon juice
300 ml (1¼ cups) custard
⅔ cup whipping
    cream*

Serves 4
Preparation time:
10–15 minutes,
plus chilling
Freezing:
Not recommended

1. Fit the metal chopping blade. Place the cherries, wine and lemon juice in the processor bowl and process for 20–30 seconds, until smooth.
2. Add the custard and process for about 5 seconds, to mix with the cherry purée. Pour into a large serving dish or individual glass dishes.
3. Whip the cream until soft peaks form, using the processor whipping blade if your model has one. Swirl into the cherry mixture to give a streaked appearance. Alternatively, pipe lines of cream onto individual servings and draw a skewer across the lines in alternate directions to create a feathered pattern. Chill thoroughly before serving.

LOGANBERRY MOUSSE

When loganberries are unavailable use raspberries instead, to make an equally delicious mousse.

350 g (12 oz) loganberries
4 tablespoons orange juice
¼–⅓ cup sugar
    (depending on
    sweetness of the fruit)
2 eggs plus 1 yolk

1 envelope gelatine
1 cup whipping cream,
    whipped
berry leaves to decorate
    (optional)

Serves 6
Preparation time:
15–20 minutes,
plus chilling
Cooking time:
5 minutes
Freezing:
Recommended

1. Place the loganberries and 1 tablespoon of the orange juice in a pan and cook gently for about 5 minutes, until just soft. Leave to cool slightly.
2. Fit the metal chopping blade. Pour the loganberry mixture into the processor bowl and process for 5–6 seconds, until smooth. Sieve to remove the pips.
3. Whisk the sugar, eggs and egg yolk together until thick; this can be done in the processor if your model has a whipping blade.
4. Sprinkle the gelatine over the remaining orange juice and leave to soften. Heat gently until dissolved, then fold into the egg mixture with the loganberry purée and half of the cream. Spoon into a serving dish and chill until set.
5. Decorate with swirls of the remaining cream and berry leaves, if available.

LEMON AND KIWI CHEESECAKE

150 g (5 oz) digestive
    biscuits
⅓ cup butter
pared rind of 1 lemon
175 g (6 oz) quark
¼ cup sugar
2 eggs, separated
1 envelope gelatine

4 tablespoons lemon juice
2 tablespoons cold water
½ cup lemon or natural
    yogurt
½ cup whipping cream
4 kiwi fruit, peeled
1 lemon

1. Grease and line a 23 cm (9 inch) loose-based cake tin.
2. Fit the metal chopping blade. Break the biscuits into the processor bowl and process for 3–5 seconds, to make crumbs.
3. Melt the butter in a pan, stir in the crumbs and mix well. Press onto the base of the prepared tin and chill until set.

4. Place the lemon rind in the processor bowl and process for 4–5 seconds, until finely chopped. Add the quark, sugar and egg yolks and process for 5–8 seconds, to blend.
5. Sprinkle the gelatine over the lemon juice and water and leave to soften, then heat gently until dissolved. Add to the cheese mixture with the yogurt and process for about 2 seconds, to blend. Transfer to a bowl and chill until just beginning to set at the edge. Wash the processor bowl.
6. Whip the cream until soft peaks form, using the processor whipping blade if your model has one. Fold into the cheesecake mixture with a metal spoon.
7. Coarsely chop one of the kiwi fruit and fold into the cheesecake mixture.
8. Whisk the egg whites until stiff peaks form, then fold into the cheesecake mixture with a metal spoon. Quickly pour onto the biscuit crust and chill until set.
9. Fit the slicing disc. Halve the lemon and slice through the disc. Slice the remaining kiwi fruit through the disc.
10. To serve, remove the cheesecake from the tin and carefully peel away the waxed paper. Decorate the top with the lemon and kiwi slices.

Serves 6–8
Preparation time: 30 minutes, plus chilling
Freezing: Recommended at end of stage 8

PINK PLUM CHIFFON

One of the simplest yet most attractive desserts I know. For maximum effect, spread the cream over the chiffon and arrange the brandy snaps on top.

540 ml (19 oz) can red
plums in syrup, drained
and stoned
1 packet raspberry jelly
150 ml (2/3 cup) boiling
water

1 cup whipping cream,
whipped
whipped cream to decorate
12 brandy snaps

Serves 6
Preparation time:
15 minutes, plus
chilling
Freezing:
Recommended

1. Fit the metal chopping blade. Place the drained plums in the processor bowl and process for 5–6 seconds, to purée.
2. Dissolve the jelly in the boiling water and mix with the plum purée. Chill until just beginning to set.
3. Return to the processor bowl with the whipped cream and process for 8–10 seconds, until foaming. Pour into a 500 g (1 lb) loaf tin and chill until set.
4. To serve, dip briefly into hot water and turn out onto a serving dish. Decorate with swirls of whipped cream and serve immediately, with brandy snaps.

ICE CREAM PROFITEROLES

*2-egg quantity Sweet
   Choux Pastry**
*about 600 ml (2½ cups)
   chocolate, vanilla or
   coffee soft scoop ice
   cream*

*CHOCOLATE SAUCE:
175 g (6 oz) plain
   chocolate
150 ml (⅔ cup) water
½ cup granulated
   sugar*

1. Place the choux pastry in a piping bag fitted with a large plain nozzle and pipe small mounds onto a greased baking sheet.
2. Bake in a preheated oven, 220°C/425°F, for 10 minutes. Lower the temperature to 190°C/375°F and bake for 20–25 minutes, until golden. Make a slit in the side of each bun to allow any steam to escape and cool on a wire rack.
3. Meanwhile, make the chocolate sauce. Place the chocolate and 3 tablespoons of the water in a pan and heat gently until melted. Add the remaining water and the sugar, blending well, and simmer, uncovered, until the chocolate coats the back of the spoon. Leave to cool.
4. Carefully spoon the ice cream into the choux buns and pile onto a serving dish. Spoon over the chocolate sauce and serve immediately.

Serves 4
Preparation time:
20–25 minutes,
plus making pastry
Cooking time:
30–35 minutes
Freezing:
Recommended;
freeze unfilled
choux buns, ice
cream and
chocolate sauce
separately

LEMON SAUCE PUDDING

A delicious tangy lemon pudding that separates into two distinctive layers after cooking—one a light lemon sponge and the other a lemon sauce.

2 tablespoons butter	*2 eggs, separated*
½ cup sugar	*½ cup all-purpose*
grated rind and juice of	*flour*
1 large lemon	*150 ml (⅔ cup) milk*

Serves 4
Preparation time:
15 minutes
Cooking time:
35 minutes
Freezing:
Not recommended

1. Fit the metal chopping or plastic blending blade. Place the butter, sugar, lemon rind and juice, egg yolks, flour and milk in the processor bowl and process for 8–10 seconds, to mix.
2. Whisk the egg whites until stiff. Fold into the lemon mixture with a metal spoon.
3. Pour into a 900 ml (3⅔ cup) pie or ovenproof dish and place in a roasting tin containing warm water to come about halfway up the dish.
4. Bake in a preheated oven, 190°C/375°F, for 35 minutes. Serve immediately, with cream if wished.

PEACH SHORTCAKE GÂTEAU

An elegant home-baked gâteau. Ring the changes by using other soft fruits in season. Best eaten on the day it is made.

50 g (2 oz) blanched	*3 tablespoons milk*
almonds	*mint sprigs to decorate*
2½ cups all-purpose flour	*FOR THE FILLING AND*
¼ cup ground rice	*TOPPING:*
1 cup butter	*1 quantity Whipped Danish*
½ cup sugar	*Cream**
finely grated rind of	*1 tablespoon icing sugar*
1 lemon	*500 g (1 lb) small peaches,*
1 egg yolk	*peeled and halved*

1. Fit the metal chopping blade. Place the almonds in the processor bowl and process for about 3 seconds, until coarsely chopped. Remove and set aside.
2. Place the flour, ground rice and butter in the processor bowl and process for about 5 seconds, until the mixture resembles fine breadcrumbs.
3. Add the almonds and remaining ingredients and process for about 4 seconds, to make a firm but pliable dough.

4. Roll out the dough on a lightly floured surface to a 25 × 18 cm (10 × 7 inch) rectangle. Cut in half to give two 25 × 9 cm (10 × 3½ inch) rectangles.
5. Place the rectangles on 1 or 2 greased baking sheets and bake in a preheated oven, 180°C/350°F, for 20–25 minutes. Cut one rectangle into 6 or 8 slices while still warm. Cool on a wire rack.
6. Meanwhile, prepare the filling and topping. Wash the processor bowl. Whip the cream with the icing sugar until soft peaks form (using the processor whipping blade if your model has one). Set aside a quarter for decoration.
7. Fit the metal chopping blade. Reserve 2 peach halves for decoration. Place the rest in the processor bowl and process for barely 1–2 seconds, until coarsely chopped. Fold into the cream.
8. Place the whole shortcake rectangle on a serving plate and spread with the peach mixture. Arrange the small shortcake slices on top.
9. Place the reserved cream in a piping bag fitted with a star-shaped nozzle and pipe a swirl of cream on each piece of shortcake.
10. Slice the reserved peach halves. Decorate the short-cake with the peach slices and mint.

Serves 6–8
Preparation time: 25 minutes, plus making cream
Cooking time: 20–25 minutes
Freezing: Recommended at end of stage 5

STRAWBERRY SHORTCAKE

2 cups all-purpose flour	2–3 tablespoons milk
1/3 cup unsalted butter	1 quantity Whipped Danish Cream*
1/4 cup sugar	500 g (1 lb) strawberries, sliced
grated rind of 1 lemon	mint leaves to decorate
1 egg, beaten	

Serves 6
Preparation time:
15 minutes, plus
making cream
Cooking time:
15–20 minutes
Freezing:
Recommended

1. Fit the metal chopping blade. Place the flour and butter in the processor bowl and process for about 5 seconds, until the mixture resembles fine breadcrumbs.

2. Add the sugar, lemon rind, egg and enough milk to process to a firm but pliable dough; process for about 4 seconds.

3. Press the mixture into a greased deep 23 cm (9 inch) fluted flan tin and level the surface. Bake just above the centre of a preheated oven, 220°C/425°F, for 15–20 minutes, until pale golden. Leave to cool in the tin for 2–3 minutes, then turn out and transfer to a wire rack and leave to cool.

4. Whip the cream until soft peaks form (using the processor whipping blade if your model has one) and pipe or spoon attractively over the cooled shortcake. Top with the strawberries and mint sprigs to serve.

VICTORIAN ICE CREAM

A popular old-fashioned favourite—a brown bread and
banana concoction in a rum-flavoured cream.

4 slices brown bread, *cubed*	*1 tablespoon rum*
	2 eggs, separated
2 ripe bananas	*½ cup cream*
¾ cup icing sugar	*1 cup whipping cream*

1. Fit the metal chopping blade. With the motor running,
add the bread cubes through the feed tube and process for
5–8 seconds, to make crumbs. Remove and set aside.
2. Place the bananas, icing sugar, rum, egg yolks and
cream in the processor bowl and process for 8–10
seconds, until smooth.
3. Whip the whipping cream until soft peaks form, using
the processor whipping blade if your model has one, then
fold into the banana mixture with the breadcrumbs.
4. Whisk the egg whites until stiff, then fold into the
mixture with a metal spoon. Pour into a rigid freezer-
proof container and freeze for 3–4 hours, until firm.
5. Transfer to the refrigerator 20 minutes before serving
to soften. Scoop into chilled glasses and serve with crisp
dessert biscuits.

Serves 4–6
Preparation time:
15 minutes, plus
freezing
Freezing:
Recommended

STRAWBERRY MOUSSE GARLAND

An elegant dessert that makes a stunning centrepiece for a summer buffet. Make 1–2 days ahead for perfect results.

3-egg quantity Victoria
 *Sandwich Mixture**
350 g (12 oz) strawberries
2 tablespoons icing sugar
2 tablespoons Cointreau
1½ teaspoons gelatine,
 soaked in 3 tablespoons
 pure orange juice
1 egg white

5 tablespoons whipping
 cream, whipped
50 g (2 oz) plain chocolate
icing sugar to dust
FOR THE MELBA SAUCE:
250 g (8 oz) raspberries
4 tablespoons icing sugar,
 sifted

Serves 8
Preparation time:
About 45 minutes, plus making cake mixture and chilling
Cooking time:
About 40 minutes
Freezing:
Recommended; freeze cake and sauce separately

1. Spoon the cake mixture into a greased 1.75 litre (7½ cup) ring mould and level the surface. Bake in a pre-heated oven, 180°C/350°F, for about 40 minutes or until well risen, golden and firm to the touch. Leave to stand in the tin for about 5 minutes, then turn out onto a wire rack to cool.

2. When cold, slice a 1 cm (½ inch) thick layer from the base of the cake and set aside. Return the rest of the cake to the washed ring mould and, using a grapefruit knife, remove the centre of the cake to leave a 1 cm (½ inch) thick shell. (Use the cut-out cake for another recipe—see Gooseberry Bakewell Tart, page 66.)

3. Fit the metal chopping blade. Place the strawberries, icing sugar and Cointreau in the processor bowl and process for about 5 seconds, to purée. Sieve to remove any seeds. Wash the processor bowl.

4. Heat the gelatine gently until dissolved, then stir into the strawberry mixture, blending well.

5. Whisk the egg white until soft peaks form, then fold into the strawberry mixture with the cream.

6. Fit the grating disc and grate the chocolate to make small curls. Fold half into the strawberry mixture.

7. Spoon into the sponge shell and cover with the reserved bottom slice. Cover and chill overnight or for at least 6–8 hours.

8. To make the melba sauce, fit the metal chopping blade. Place the raspberries in the processor bowl and process for about 5 seconds, to purée. Sieve to remove any seeds, then gradually beat in the icing sugar. Chill.

9. To serve, unmould the cake onto a serving plate. Dust with a little icing sugar and sprinkle with the remaining chocolate curls. Serve with the melba sauce.

LEMON AND GINGER SALAD

2 crisp apples, cored and
    quartered
1 pear, cored and
    quartered
125 g (4 oz) strawberries
2 peaches, quartered
1 banana
284 ml (10 oz) can lychees,
    drained

125 g (4 oz) black grapes,
    halved and seeded
FOR THE SYRUP:
5 cm (2 inch) piece fresh
    root ginger
1 small lemon, halved
1 cup sugar
150 ml (2/3 cup) water

1. First prepare the syrup. Fit the metal chopping blade. Place the ginger in the processor bowl and process for about 5 seconds, until finely chopped. Place in a pan.
2. Fit the slicing disc and slice the lemon. Add to the pan with the sugar and water. Heat gently until the sugar has dissolved, bring to the boil, then simmer for 5 minutes. Leave to cool.
3. Meanwhile, slice the apples, pear, strawberries, peaches and banana through the disc and place in a serving dish. Add the lychees and grapes, stirring to mix.
4. Strain the syrup over the fruit salad and toss gently to mix. Serve lightly chilled, with cream if you wish.

Serves 4–6
Preparation time:
20 minutes, plus
cooling time
Cooking time:
About 10 minutes
Freezing:
Recommended

ST CLEMENT'S BEIGNETS

Light-as-air deep-fried choux pastry pieces sprinkled with sugar and served with an orange and lemon sauce make an elegant, if somewhat indulgent, dessert.

*2-egg quantity Sweet
    Choux Pastry**
sugar to sprinkle
FOR THE SAUCE:
*thinly pared rind of
    ½ lemon*
*thinly pared rind of
    ¼ orange*

⅓ cup sugar
1 teaspoon corn starch
300 ml (1¼ cups) water
2 tablespoons butter
1 tablespoon lemon juice
3 tablespoons orange juice

Serves 4
Preparation time:
20 minutes, plus
making pastry
Cooking time:
About 15 minutes
Freezing:
Not recommended

1. First prepare the sauce. Fit the metal chopping blade. Place the lemon and orange rinds in the processor bowl and process for 5–8 seconds, until finely chopped.
2. Mix the sugar with the corn starch in a pan. Gradually add the water, blending well, bring to the boil, stirring, and cook until clear and thickened. Stir in the butter, lemon and orange rind and juice. Simmer for 5 minutes. Keep warm.
3. Place the choux pastry in a piping bag fitted with a fluted nozzle and carefully pipe small pieces into hot oil in a deep pan. Deep-fry for 3–5 minutes, until golden.
4. Drain on kitchen paper and sprinkle with sugar. Serve immediately, with the sauce.

GOOSEBERRY HONEY CHARLOTTE

A sumptuous summer dessert—special enough to present at a dinner party or buffet.

250 g (8 oz) gooseberries
*1–2 tablespoons pure
    orange juice*
*1 envelope gelatine, soaked
    in 3 tablespoons water*
300 ml (1¼ cups) milk
3 egg yolks
4 tablespoons clear honey
1 teaspoon lemon juice

*about 16 sponge fingers or
    langue de chat biscuits*
3 tablespoons sweet sherry
½ cup whipping cream
1 egg white
*whipped cream to decorate
    (optional)*

1. Cook the gooseberries gently in the orange juice for about 10 minutes, or until tender.

2. Fit the metal chopping blade. Place the gooseberries and their liquid in the processor bowl and process for 5–6 seconds, until smooth. Remove and set aside.

3. Heat the gelatine gently until dissolved.

4. Heat the milk to just below boiling point. Beat the egg yolks and honey together, then stir into the milk. Cook gently, stirring constantly, until the custard coats the back of the spoon. Stir in the gelatine, gooseberry purée and lemon juice. Strain into a bowl and chill until on the point of setting.

5. Briefly dip the sponge fingers or biscuits in the sherry and use to line the side of a 1.2 litre (5 cup) charlotte or fluted jelly mould.

6. Whip the cream until soft peaks form (using the processor whipping blade if your model has one). Fold into the gooseberry mixture with a metal spoon.

7. Whisk the egg white until stiff peaks form, then fold into the gooseberry mixture. Spoon into the biscuit-lined mould and chill until set.

8. To serve, dip briefly into hot water, and carefully unmould the charlotte onto a serving plate. Decorate with swirls of whipped cream, if you wish.

Serves 6–8
Preparation time:
30 minutes, plus chilling
Cooking time:
20 minutes
Freezing:
Recommended

TROPICAL CHRISTMAS CAKE

This exotic ring-shaped Christmas cake—laden with dried fruits, nuts and pineapple—has a coconut and pineapple frosting. Finish with a colourful ribbon if you wish.

284 ml (10 oz) can
  pineapple slices in
  natural juice, drained
  and juice reserved
3/4 cup butter
1/2 cup sugar
2 extra large eggs
2 cups all-purpose
  flour
75 g (3 oz) glacé cherries,
  quartered
75 g (3 oz) chopped mixed
  peel

125 g (4 oz) raisins
1/4 cup shredded
  coconut
25 g (1 oz) angelica,
  chopped
25 g (1 oz) walnut pieces
FOR THE FROSTING:
1/4 cup butter
1 1/3 cups icing sugar
1/4 cup shredded
  coconut
TO DECORATE:
glacé fruits and angelica

**Makes one
1.5 litre
(6 cup)
ring cake
Preparation time:**
30–40 minutes
Cooking time:
About 1 hour
Freezing:
Not recommended

1. Fit the metal chopping blade. Place the pineapple in the processor bowl and process for 2–3 seconds, until finely chopped. Remove and set aside.

2. Place the butter, sugar, eggs, flour and 3 tablespoons of the reserved pineapple juice in the processor bowl and process for about 20 seconds, until well blended.

3. Transfer to a mixing bowl and fold in the pineapple, cherries, peel, raisins, coconut, angelica and walnut pieces; it is better to do this by hand as most processors cannot cope with such a large quantity, but if you have a catering size processor, process for 3–4 seconds.

4. Spoon into a greased 1.5 litre (6 cup) ring mould and bake in a preheated oven, 170°C/325°F, for about 1 hour, until a skewer pierced through the centre of the cake comes out clean. Leave to cool in the tin for 15 minutes, then transfer to a wire rack.

5. To make the frosting, melt the butter in a pan. Stir in the icing sugar, coconut and 1 tablespoon of the reserved pineapple juice. Spread quickly over the cake and decorate with glacé fruits and angelica as you wish.

SPICED APPLE CAKE

This moist, spiced apple cake is delicious served cold, dusted with icing sugar. It can also be served as a warm pudding with whipped cream.

500 g (1 lb) apples,
*   peeled and cored*
2 cups all-purpose flour
1/2 teaspoon ground cloves
1/4 teaspoon grated
*   nutmeg*

1/2 cup soft margarine
250 g (8 oz) sugar
2 eggs
1/4 cup walnut pieces
sifted icing sugar to dust

Makes one 20 cm (8 inch) round cake
Preparation time:
15–20 minutes
Cooking time:
1½ hours
Freezing:
Not recommended

1. Grease and line a deep 20 cm (8 inch) round cake tin.
2. Fit the slicing disc and slice the apples. Remove and set aside. Wash the processor bowl.
3. Fit the metal chopping blade. Place the flour, cloves and nutmeg in the processor bowl and process for about 1 second, to sift. Add the margarine, sugar and eggs and process for 10–12 seconds, until well blended. Add the walnuts and process for 1–2 seconds, to mix.
4. Spoon half of the cake mixture into the prepared tin and spread evenly. Cover with the apple slices, then top with the remaining cake mixture; do not worry too much about spreading evenly, as the mixture will cover the apples during cooking.
5. Bake in a preheated oven, 170°C/325°F, for about 1½ hours, until well risen, golden and a skewer pierced through the centre of the cake comes out clean. Leave to cool in the tin if serving cold.
6. Transfer to a serving plate and dust with icing sugar.

GINGERBREAD SLICES

This delicious moist gingerbread is best allowed to mature for a few days before eating.

4 cups all-purpose flour
3 teaspoons ground ginger
3 teaspoons baking
*   powder*
1 teaspoon baking soda
1 teaspoon salt
1 cup demerara sugar

3/4 cup unsalted butter
1/2 cup molasses
1/2 cup golden syrup
300 ml (1 1/4 cups) milk
1 egg, beaten

1. Grease and line a deep 23 cm (9 inch) square cake tin.
2. Fit the metal chopping or plastic blending blade. Place the flour, ginger, baking powder, baking soda and salt in the processor bowl and process for about 3 seconds, to sift.
3. Place the sugar, butter, molasses and syrup in a pan and heat gently until melted.
4. With the motor running, pour the butter mixture, milk and egg through the feed tube and process for 8–10 seconds, until well blended.
5. Pour into the prepared tin and bake in a preheated oven, 180°C/350°F, for about 1½ hours or until well risen and just firm to the touch.
6. Leave to cool in the tin for 15 minutes, then turn out onto a wire rack. When completely cold, wrap in foil, without removing the waxed paper, and store for 4–7 days to mature. Cut into slices to serve.

Makes one 23 cm (9 inch) square cake
Preparation time: 15 minutes
Cooking time: 1½ hours
Freezing: Recommended

HONEY CARROT CAKE

4 large carrots
2 cups all-purpose
flour
¹/₂ teaspoon salt
³/₄ teaspoon baking soda
1 teaspoon baking powder
¹/₂ teaspoon ground
cinnamon
¹/₂ cup granulated
sugar
3 tablespoons set honey
2 eggs, beaten
5 tablespoons oil

398 ml (14 oz) can
crushed pineapple,
drained
¹/₄ cup walnut pieces
FOR THE FROSTING:
1³/₄ cups icing sugar
¹/₄ cup butter
¹/₄ cup cream cheese
¹/₂ teaspoon vanilla
extract
1–2 teaspoons milk
TO DECORATE:
walnut halves

**Makes one 18 cm
(7 inch) round
cake
Preparation time:**
20 minutes
Cooking time:
35–40 minutes
Freezing:
Not recommended

1. Grease and line a deep 18 cm (7 inch) round cake tin.
2. Fit the grating disc and grate the carrots. Set aside.
3. Fit the metal chopping blade. Place the flour, salt, baking soda, baking powder, cinnamon and sugar in the processor bowl and process for 3–4 seconds, to sift.
4. Add the honey, eggs, oil, pineapple, walnuts and grated carrot and process for 8–10 seconds, to mix.
5. Pour the mixture into the prepared tin and bake in a preheated oven, 180°C/350°F, for 35–40 minutes. Cool on a wire rack.
6. To make the frosting, place the ingredients in the processor bowl and process for 10 seconds, until smooth.
7. Spread and swirl over the top and side of the cake. Decorate with walnut halves to serve.

HAZELNUT AND BANANA TEA LOAF

The addition of bananas gives this a good moist texture and excellent keeping quality. Serve plain or buttered.

¹/₃ cup hazelnuts
2 bananas
¹/₂ cup butter
³/₄ cup light brown
sugar

2 eggs
2 cups all-purpose
flour
1 teaspoon baking powder
2 tablespoons milk

1. Grease and line a 1 kg (2 lb) loaf tin.
2. Fit the metal chopping blade. Place the hazelnuts in the processor bowl and process for about 3 seconds, until coarsely chopped. Remove and set aside.

3. Place the bananas in the processor bowl and process for about 4 seconds, until smooth. Remove and set aside. Wash the processor bowl.

4. Place the butter, sugar, eggs, flour, baking powder and milk in the processor bowl and process for about 10 seconds, until well blended. Add the bananas and hazelnuts and process for 1–2 seconds, to mix.

5. Spoon into the prepared tin and level the surface. Bake in a preheated oven, 180°C/350°F, for about 1 hour or until the loaf is well risen, golden brown and firm to the touch. Turn out onto a wire rack to cool.

Makes one 1 kg (2 lb) loaf
Preparation time: 15 minutes
Cooking time: 1 hour
Freezing: Recommended

ORANGE AND ALMOND LOAF

A rich fruit and nut teatime loaf that will keep in an airtight container for 2–3 weeks.

500 g (1 lb) raisins
²/₃ cup tropical fruit
  juice
125 g (4 oz) blanched
  almonds
3 cups all-purpose flour

¹/₄ cup butter
2 oranges
¹/₄ cup sugar
3 tablespoons milk
2 eggs

**Makes one 1 kg
(2 lb) loaf
Preparation time:**
20 minutes
Cooking time:
About 1 hour
Freezing:
Recommended

1. Fit the metal chopping blade. Place the raisins in the processor bowl and process for 2–4 seconds, until coarsely chopped. Place in a pan with the tropical fruit juice, bring slowly to the boil, then remove from the heat and set aside.

2. Place the almonds in the processor bowl and process for about 2 seconds, until coarsely chopped. Remove and set aside.

3. Place the flour and butter in the processor bowl and process for 7–8 seconds, until the mixture resembles fine breadcrumbs.

4. Finely grate the orange rinds, discard the pith and chop the flesh.

5. Add the sugar, almonds, raisin mixture, milk, eggs and orange rind to the processor bowl and process for 8–10 seconds, until well blended. Add the orange flesh and process for 1–2 seconds, to mix.

6. Pour into a greased 1 kg (2 lb) loaf tin and bake in a preheated oven, 180°C/350°F, for about 1 hour. Cool on a wire rack and cut into thin slices to serve.

HARVEST VICTORIA CAKE

A Victoria sponge cake with a delicious difference—the top is baked with a colourful fruit and nut topping.

grated rind of 2 lemons
2-egg quantity Victoria
  Sandwich Mixture*
2 tablespoons quartered
  coloured glacé cherries
1 tablespoon chopped
  mixed peel

15 g (¹/₂ oz) slivered
  almonds
FOR THE BUTTERCREAM:
1 cup icing sugar,
  sifted
¹/₄ cup butter
1 tablespoon lemon juice

1. Grease and base-line two 18 cm (7 inch) cake pans.
2. Add the lemon rind to the prepared cake mixture in the processor bowl and process for 1–2 seconds, to mix.
3. Divide the mixture between the prepared cake pans and smooth the tops. Sprinkle one cake evenly with the glacé cherries, peel and almonds.
4. Bake in a preheated oven, 180°C/350°F, for 25–30 minutes or until the tops spring back when lightly pressed. Leave to cool in the tins for 2–3 minutes, then transfer to a wire rack.
5. Meanwhile, wash the processor bowl and fit the metal chopping or plastic blending blade. Place the icing sugar, butter and lemon juice in the processor bowl and process for about 5 seconds, until smooth.
6. To serve, sandwich the cakes together with the lemon buttercream, placing the fruit-topped cake on top.

Makes one 18 cm (7 inch) cake
Preparation time: 10–15 minutes, plus making cake mixture
Cooking time: 25–30 minutes
Freezing: Recommended

GOOSEBERRY BAKEWELL TART

.This is a scrumptious tart to make when you have a little left-over plain cake to crumb. Once cut, the rich, crisp and golden topping reveals the gooey jam filling.

*250 g (8 oz) Shortcrust
    Pastry**
*3 tablespoons gooseberry
    jam*
FOR THE TOPPING:
*75 g (3 oz) Madeira or
    other plain cake*
¼ cup butter

¼ cup sugar
grated rind of ½ lemon
1 extra large egg
¾ cup ground almonds
*1 tablespoon lemon juice
    or milk*
icing sugar to dust

Serves 6
Preparation time:
25 minutes, plus
making pastry
Cooking time:
30–40 minutes
Freezing:
Recommended

1. Roll out the pastry on a lightly floured surface and use to line a 20 cm (8 inch) loose-based flan tin or a deep pie plate. Trim and flute the edges of the pie plate, if using.
2. Spread the jam evenly over the pastry base.
3. To make the topping, fit the metal chopping blade, place the cake in the processor bowl and process for about 3 seconds, to make fine crumbs. Add the butter, sugar, lemon rind, egg, almonds and lemon juice or milk and process for 10–12 seconds, until well blended.
4. Spread the topping evenly over the gooseberry jam and smooth the surface.
5. Bake in a preheated oven, 200°C/400°F, for 30–40 minutes or until well risen, golden and firm to the touch.
6. Serve warm or cold, dusted with a little icing sugar.

FRUIT AND CINNAMON SCONES

Healthy and wholesome, fruit and cinnamon scones can be made with almost any combination of dried fruits, including apricots, raisins and those suggested here. The quantities below give excellent results.

*⅓ cup mixed dried
    banana, pear and apple
    pieces*
1 dried fig, halved
2 cups whole wheat flour
pinch of salt
*1 tablespoon baking
    powder*

*½ teaspoon ground
    cinnamon*
¼ cup butter
2 tablespoons sugar
150 ml (⅔ cup) milk
milk to glaze

1. Fit the metal chopping blade. Place the banana, pear, apple and fig in the processor bowl and process for 3–5 seconds, until coarsely chopped. Remove and set aside.
2. Place the flour, salt, baking powder, cinnamon and butter in the processor bowl and process for about 5 seconds, until the mixture resembles fine breadcrumbs.
3. Add the sugar and dried fruit. With the motor running, add the milk through the feed tube and process for 4–6 seconds, to make a soft dough. Turn onto a lightly floured surface and knead until smooth.
4. Roll out to about a 1 cm (½ inch) thickness and cut out 12 rounds using a 5 cm (2 inch) cutter. Place on a greased baking sheet and brush with milk.
5. Bake in a preheated oven, 220°C/425°F, for 8–10 minutes or until well risen and golden. Cool on a wire rack.

Makes 12
Preparation time:
10–15 minutes
Cooking time:
8–10 minutes
Freezing:
Recommended

FARMHOUSE FESTIVAL LOAF

Homemade bread can become an everyday luxury, especially if you mix and knead the dough in the processor, then leave it to prove slowly overnight in the refrigerator ready for baking the following morning.

15 g (¹/₂ oz) fresh yeast
¹/₂ teaspoon molasses
⁷/₈ cup warm water
3 cups whole wheat flour

¹/₂ teaspoon salt
1¹/₂ teaspoons sunflower oil
buckwheat, cracked wheat, seeds or nuts to sprinkle (optional)

Makes one 500 g (1 lb) loaf
Preparation time: 30 minutes, plus rising time
Cooking time: 15–30 minutes
Freezing: Recommended

1. Cream the yeast and molasses with a third of the water. Leave in a warm place for about 5 minutes, until frothy.
2. Fit the metal chopping blade. Place the flour, salt and oil in the processor bowl. With the motor running, add the yeast liquid and remaining water through the feed tube; process for 30 seconds, to blend and knead the dough.
3. Cover the processor bowl with plastic wrap and leave to rise in a warm place for 1¹/₂–2 hours, until doubled in size.
4. Process for about 10–15 seconds, to knock back and knead the dough.
5. Flatten the dough out to an oblong about 2.5 cm (1 inch) thick. Fold into three, like an envelope, and tuck the 2 short ends over the seam to fit the tin. Place seam-side down in a greased 500 g (1 lb) loaf tin.
6. Cover with plastic wrap and leave to rise in a warm place for 30 minutes to 1 hour, until almost doubled in size. Sprinkle with buckwheat, cracked wheat, seeds or nuts, or a combination, if you wish.
7. Bake in a preheated oven, 220°C/425°F, for 25–30 minutes, until the bread sounds hollow when tapped underneath. Turn out and cool on a wire rack.

VARIATIONS

Plait: Divide the dough into 3 equal pieces. Roll each into a long strand and plait them loosely together, starting in the centre and working to each end in turn. Dampen the ends and pinch together to seal. Place on a greased baking sheet and proceed as above.

Cloverleaf Rolls: Divide the dough into 6 equal portions, then divide each into 3 pieces. Shape each piece into a small ball. Place in groups of 3 on a greased baking sheet and proceed as above, cooking for 15–20 minutes.

BEAN BURGERS

250 g (8 oz) lean beef
1/2 teaspoon French
     mustard
1 tablespoon chopped
     parsley
213 ml (7 1/2 oz) can baked
     beans
salt and pepper to taste

oil for brushing
TO SERVE:
4 small whole grain ham-
     burger buns, halved
     and lightly toasted
4 lettuce leaves
2 tomatoes, sliced
tomato ketchup (optional)

Serves 4
Preparation time:
15 minutes, plus
chilling
Cooking time:
10 minutes
Freezing:
Recommended at
end of stage 2, if
fresh meat used

1. Fit the metal chopping blade. Place the beef in the processor bowl and process for 5–6 seconds, to grind. Add the mustard, parsley, beans, and salt and pepper, and process for 2–3 seconds, to mix.
2. Divide and shape into 4 burgers and chill for 1 hour.
3. Brush with oil and cook under a broiler for 5 minutes on each side. Serve in a bun, with lettuce, tomato, and ketchup if you wish.

ALL SEASONS MEATLOAF

4 slices whole wheat
     bread, cubed
1 onion
500 g (1 lb) chuck or
     braising steak
250 g (8 oz) diced
     shoulder pork

50 g (2 oz) mushrooms
1 tablespoon tomato paste
1 egg
150 ml (2/3 cup) vegetable
     stock or tomato juice

Serves 8
Preparation time:
15 minutes
Cooking time:
About 1 1/2 hours
Freezing:
Recommended

1. Fit the metal chopping blade. With the motor running, add the bread cubes through the feed tube and process to make crumbs. Remove and set aside.
2. Place the onion in the processor bowl and process for 4–5 seconds, until finely chopped. Remove and set aside.
3. Place the steak and pork in the processor bowl and process for 8–10 seconds, to grind. Add all the remaining ingredients and process for 5–7 seconds, until well mixed.
4. Spoon into a greased 1 kg (2 lb) loaf tin, press down firmly and cover with foil. Bake in a preheated oven, 180°C/350°F, for about 1 1/2 hours, until firm.
5. Turn out and slice, then serve with vegetables or salad.

COTTAGE ONE-POTS

An ideal dinner for older babies and toddlers—well worth
keeping a supply in the freezer.

1 bacon slice
1 onion
1 celery stick
1 large carrot
500 g (1 lb) braising lamb
1 tablespoon oil
213 ml (7½ oz) can
  tomatoes, chopped

4 tablespoons meat or
  vegetable stock
500 g (1 lb) potatoes,
  boiled
½ cup cottage cheese
1–2 tablespoons milk

Serves 6–8
Preparation time:
25–30 minutes
Cooking time:
15–20 minutes
Freezing:
Recommended
for up to 3 months

1. Fit the metal chopping blade. Place the bacon in the
processor bowl and process for 2–3 seconds, to chop.
2. Add the onion, celery and carrot and process for about
5 seconds, to chop. Remove and set aside.
3. Place the lamb in the processor bowl and process for
8–10 seconds, to mince. Remove and set aside. Wash the
processor bowl
4. Heat the oil in a pan, add the bacon and vegetable
mixture and fry for 5 minutes. Add the lamb and cook for
about 10 minutes, until lightly browned.
5. Stir in the tomatoes with their juice and the stock.
Simmer for about 15 minutes, until thickened. Divide
between 6–8 ramekins or small ovenproof dishes.
6. Fit the metal chopping blade. Place the potatoes, cottage cheese and milk in the processor bowl and process
for 4–6 seconds, until a smooth purée forms; time carefully, making sure not to over-process. Spoon or pipe
attractively over the lamb mixture.
7. Bake in a preheated oven, 200°C/400°F, for 15–20
minutes, until golden.

NUT AND OAT SLICES

½ cup butter
¼ cup dark brown
  sugar
2 eggs
2 tablespoons milk
¾ cup whole wheat
  flour
2 teaspoons baking
  powder

¾ cup quick rolled oats
3 tablespoons natural
  bran
½ cup walnut pieces
FOR THE FROSTING:
½ cup cream cheese
2 teaspoons icing sugar
3 tablespoons orange juice

1. Grease and line a shallow 20 cm (8 inch) square cake tin.

2. Fit the metal chopping or plastic blending blade. Place the butter, sugar, eggs, milk, flour, baking powder, oats and bran in the processor bowl and process for 10–12 seconds, until well blended. Add the walnuts and process for 1–2 seconds, to mix.

3. Spoon into the prepared tin and spread evenly. Bake in a preheated oven, 190°C/375°F, for 20–25 minutes, or until firm but springy to the touch. Leave to cool slightly in the tin, then turn out onto a wire rack.

4. To make the frosting, fit the metal chopping or plastic blending blade. Place all the ingredients in the cleaned processor bowl and process for about 5 seconds, until smooth.

5. Swirl the frosting over the cooled cake with a palette knife. Cut into slices to serve.

Makes 16
Preparation time:
20–25 minutes
Cooking time:
20–25 minutes
Freezing:
Not recommended

FRUIT YOGURT JELLIES

These fruit jellies are perfect for packed lunches—simply cover with plastic wrap.

1 envelope gelatine
300 ml (1¼ cups) red
*   grape juice*
150 g (5 oz) raspberries

1¼ cups raspberry
*   yogurt*
few raspberries to decorate

Makes 4–6
Preparation time:
10 minutes, plus chilling
Freezing:
Not recommended

1. Sprinkle the gelatine over the grape juice and leave to soften. Heat gently in a pan until dissolved.
2. Fit the metal chopping blade. Place the grape juice, raspberries and yogurt in the processor bowl and process for about 5 seconds, to blend.
3. Pour into individual dishes, pots or jelly moulds and chill until set.
4. If using jelly moulds, dip briefly into hot water and turn out onto small plates. Decorate with a few whole raspberries to serve.

TROPICAL FRUIT DESSERT

An exotic selection of tropical fruits puréed together to make a delicious dessert, suitable for the very young, and popular with older children too. Serve one portion and freeze the remainder. As a guide, very early weaners will probably eat 1 cube per serving, babies from 4–6 months may need 2 cubes, and those aged 6–9 months should be offered 3 cubes.

1 large ripe banana
175 g (6 oz) piece melon

½ guava, mango or
papaya, peeled and
stoned or seeded

1. Fit the metal chopping blade. Place all the fruit in the processor bowl and process for 3–5 seconds, until smooth. Sieve to remove any seeds if necessary.
2. Serve one portion immediately. Spoon the remainder into deep ice cube trays, overwrap in foil and freeze until firm. Thaw thoroughly to serve.

Makes about 30 cubes
Preparation time: 5–10 minutes
Freezing: Recommended for up to 1 month

VARIATIONS
Replace the guava, mango or papaya with 1 ripe pear; 5 tablespoons cooked apple; 125 g (4 oz) strawberries; a large peeled peach; or 2–3 peeled apricots.

COTTAGE CHEESE FRUIT SAVOURY

This is a first 'solid' fruit savoury for the very young —introduce at about 3–4 months. See above for serving guidelines. If you prefer, replace the mango with a large ripe papaya or 2 small bananas.

1 large mango, peeled
½ cup cottage cheese

5 tablespoons natural
pineapple juice
1 teaspoon clear honey
(optional)

1. Fit the metal chopping blade. Place the mango flesh in the processor bowl and process for about 2 seconds, to chop.
2. Add the cottage cheese, pineapple juice and honey, if using, and process for 2 seconds, until smooth.
3. Serve immediately; spoon the remainder into deep ice cube trays, overwrap in foil and freeze until firm. Thaw thoroughly to serve.

Makes about 20 cubes
Preparation time: 5–10 minutes
Freezing: Recommended for up to 2 months

BASIC RECIPES

BASIC BATTER

This quantity is sufficient to make one large Yorkshire pudding or toad-in-the-hole or about 8 medium pancakes.

1 cup all-purpose flour
pinch of salt
1 egg

1 tablespoon oil
300 ml (1¼ cups) milk, or
milk and water mixed

**Makes about
300 ml (1¼ cups)**
Preparation time:
5 minutes
Freezing:
Not recommended

1. Fit the metal chopping or plastic blending blade. Place the flour, salt, egg, oil and half of the liquid in the processor bowl and process for about 15 seconds, to mix.
2. Add the remaining liquid and process for 15 seconds. Use as required.

CHOUX PASTRY

Choux pastry is perhaps one of the most intriguing pastries because it hardly looks like a pastry at all until cooked. Simple to make, it is used for éclairs, gougères, profiteroles and sweet or savoury filled puffs. This quantity makes sufficient for 25–30 profiteroles, 10 éclairs, 1 puff ring or gougère or 10 small puffs.

⅔ cup all-purpose flour
pinch of salt

¼ cup butter, diced
150 ml (⅔ cup) water
2 eggs

**Makes a 2-egg
quantity**
Preparation time:
10–15 minutes
Freezing:
Recommended;
shape and freeze
before baking

1. Fit the metal chopping blade. Place the flour and salt in the processor bowl and process for about 1 second, to sift.
2. Place the butter and water in a pan, heat slowly to melt the butter, then bring to a fast boil.
3. With the motor running, quickly add to the processor bowl through the feed tube and process for about 3 seconds, to blend.
4. Add the eggs, one at a time, and process until thick and glossy. Use as required.

VARIATION
Sweet Choux Pastry: Prepare as above, adding 1 teaspoon sugar to the water and butter mixture.

SHORTCRUST PASTRY

A quick and easy one-stage pastry suitable for pies, flans and tarts. This quantity is sufficient for a 20 cm (8 inch) flan, 12 double-crust tartlets, 4 small Cornish pasties or 1 large pie crust.

2 cups all-purpose flour	*¼ cup butter, diced*
¼ teaspoon salt	*¼ cup shortening, diced*
	2 tablespoons iced water

1. Fit the metal chopping blade. Place the flour, salt, butter and shortening in the processor bowl and process for 7–8 seconds, until the mixture resembles fine breadcrumbs.
2. With the motor running, add the water slowly through the feed tube and process until the ingredients just bind together to make a ball.
3. Turn onto a lightly floured surface and knead until smooth. Wrap in foil or plastic wrap and chill for 15 minutes before using.

Makes 250 g (8 oz)
Preparation time: 5 minutes, plus chilling
Freezing: Recommended

VARIATIONS

Whole wheat Shortcrust Pastry: Use whole wheat flour instead of all-purpose flour, and 2–3 tablespoons iced water.

Cheese Shortcrust Pastry: Fit the grating disc and grate 75 g (3 oz) Cheddar cheese. Remove and set aside. Fit the metal chopping blade. Prepare as above, but add ½ teaspoon mustard powder with the flour, and the grated cheese with the water.

Rich Sweet Shortcrust Pastry: Fit the metal chopping blade. Place 1½ cups all-purpose flour, ⅓ cup diced butter and 2 tablespoons sugar in the processor bowl and process as above. With the motor running, add 1 egg yolk and 1 tablespoon iced water through the feed tube and process as above.

Nut Shortcrust Pastry: Prepare as above, adding ¼ cup chopped nuts with the iced water.

Herby Shortcrust Pastry: Prepare as above, adding 1½–2 teaspoons dried herbs with the flour.

Lemon Shortcrust Pastry: Prepare as above, adding the grated rind of ½ lemon with the flour.

HOT WATER CRUST PASTRY

A crisp rich pastry used to make raised pies and picnic or buffet table fare. This quantity is sufficient for a 500 g (1 lb) loaf-shaped pie, a 15 cm (6 inch) round pie or 4 individual double-crust pies.

3 cups all-purpose flour　　*½ cup lard, diced*
1 teaspoon salt　　　　　　*150 ml (²/₃ cup) water, or*
　　　　　　　　　　　　　　milk and water mixed

**Makes 350 g
(12 oz)
Preparation time:**
10–15 minutes
Freezing:
Not recommended

1. Fit the metal chopping blade. Place the flour and salt in the processor bowl and process for about 1 second, to sift.
2. Place the lard and liquid in a pan, heat slowly to melt the lard, then bring to a fast boil.
3. With the motor running, quickly add to the processor bowl through the feed tube and process for about 3 seconds, to blend.
4. Turn onto a lightly floured surface and knead until smooth. Use as required, while still warm.

VARIATION

Whole wheat Hot Water Crust Pastry: Use whole wheat flour instead of all-purpose and increase the liquid to 225 ml (⅞ cup).

WHIPPED DANISH CREAM

A useful cream made with butter, milk and gelatine. It produces a cream with a thick pouring consistency which can be whipped lightly to form soft peaks.

½ cup unsalted　　　　*½ teaspoon gelatine,*
　butter, diced　　　　　*soaked in 2 teaspoons*
150 ml (²/₃ cup) milk　　*cold water*
　　　　　　　　　　　　1–2 teaspoons sugar
　　　　　　　　　　　　(optional)

**Makes 300 ml
(1¼ cups)
Preparation time:**
10–15 minutes,
plus chilling
Freezing:
Not recommended

1. Place the butter and milk in a pan and heat gently until melted; do not allow to boil.
2. Add a little of the milk to the gelatine and stir well. Return to the pan with the sugar, if using, blending well.
3. Fit the metal chopping, plastic blending or whipping blade. Pour the cream mixture into the processor bowl and process for 30 seconds. Pour into a bowl and chill for 3–4 hours or overnight. Use as required.

VICTORIA SANDWICH MIXTURE

Light, spongy and endlessly versatile, this one-stage Victoria sandwich mixture will prove invaluable for making small cakes, large elaborate gâteaux and speedy sponge-topped fruit puddings. This quantity is sufficient for an 18 cm (7 inch) cake.

1 cup all-purpose flour
³⁄₄ teaspoon baking
    powder

¹⁄₂ cup soft margarine
¹⁄₂ cup sugar
2 eggs

Makes a 2-egg quantity
Preparation time: 10–15 minutes
Freezing: Recommended when baked

Fit the metal chopping or plastic blending blade. Place all the ingredients in the processor bowl and process for 10–12 seconds, until well blended. Use as required.

MAYONNAISE

3 egg yolks
¹⁄₂ teaspoon salt
¹⁄₂ teaspoon mustard
    powder
pinch of cayenne pepper

5 teaspoons white wine
    vinegar or lemon juice
300 ml (1¹⁄₄ cups) olive or
    other salad oil

Makes about 300 ml (1¹⁄₄ cups)
Preparation time: 5 minutes
Freezing: Not recommended

1. Fit the metal chopping blade. Place the egg yolks, salt, mustard powder, cayenne pepper and 3 teaspoons of the vinegar or lemon juice in the processor bowl and process for about 3 seconds, to blend.
2. With the motor running, add the oil in a steady stream through the feed tube and process until thick and glossy.
3. Add the remaining vinegar or lemon juice and process for about 1 second, to blend. Use as required.

VARIATIONS
Use tarragon, cider or herb vinegar for a change.

Garlic Mayonnaise: Prepare as above, adding ¹⁄₂–1 teaspoon garlic purée (see page 6) with the final vinegar.

Green or Herb Mayonnaise: Fit the metal chopping blade. Place 2 green onions, 3 parsley sprigs, 1 tarragon sprig and a few chives in the processor bowl and process until finely chopped. Remove and set aside. Prepare the mayonnaise as above, adding the herbs with the final vinegar.

INDEX

Photography by: Martin Brigdale
Designed by: Sue Storey
Home economist: Lyn Rutherford
Stylist: Alison Williams
Illustration by: Linda Smith
Typeset by Rowland Phototypesetting Ltd